Career Discovery Encyclopedia

Seventh Edition

EDITORIAL STAFF

EDITORIAL DIRECTOR
Laurie Likoff

EDITOR IN CHIEF
James Chambers

CONTRIBUTOR, "Finding a Career That's Right for You"
Maurene J. Hinds

MANUSCRIPT EDITORS
Rayna Bailey
Pamela Fehl
Angie Miccinello

PROOFREADING
Vanessa Leahey

INDEXING
Columbia Indexing Group

Career Discovery Encyclopedia

Seventh Edition

VOLUME 7

Pop and Rock Musicians
Sports Equipment Managers

Ferguson
An imprint of Infobase Publishing

Career Discovery Encyclopedia, Seventh Edition

Ferguson
An imprint of Infobase Publishing
132 West 31st Street
New York NY 10001

Library of Congress Cataloging-in-Publication Data

Career discovery encyclopedia. — 7th ed.
    v. cm.
 Includes index.
 ISBN-13: 978-0-8160-7931-5 (hardcover : alk. paper)
 ISBN-10: 0-8160-7931-5 (hardcover : alk. paper) 1. Vocational guidance—Dictionaries, Juvenile. I. Ferguson Publishing.
 HF5381.2.C37 2009
 331.70203—dc22
                           2009003162

Ferguson books are available at special discounts when purchased in bulk quantities for businesses, associations, institutions, or sales promotions. Please call our Special Sales Department in New York at (212) 967-8800 or (800) 322-8755.

You can find Ferguson on the World Wide Web at http://www.fergpubco.com

Text design adapted by Kerry Casey
Cover design by Alicia Post

Printed in the United States of America

Bang EJB 10 9 8 7 6 5 4 3 2 1

This book is printed on acid-free paper.

Contents

Career Cluster Icons

Agriculture, Food, and Natural Resources

Hospitality and Tourism

Architecture and Construction

Human Services

Arts, Audio-Video Technology, and Communication

Information Technology

Business, Management, and Administration

Law, Public Safety, and Security

Education and Training

Manufacturing

Finance

Marketing, Sales, and Service

Government and Public Administration

Science, Technology, Engineering, and Mathematics

Health Science

Transportation, Distribution, and Logistics

CAREER ARTICLES

Pop and Rock Musicians

What Pop and Rock Musicians Do

Pop and rock musicians perform in clubs, in concert halls, on college campuses, and at festivals and fairs. They often write original music and perform it with other instrumentalists and vocalists. They may record their music for sale.

After writing the music, musicians spend many hours rehearsing new songs with other band members. Many pop and rock musicians record a demo (demonstration), which they send to club managers and music producers. When making a demo tape or recording a CD for a record company, they record in a studio and work with recording professionals, such as audio engineers, producers, and mixing engineers. Musicians may also have to audition live for a club manager in addition to providing a demo tape.

When a club books a band, the club's promotional staff may advertise the upcoming performance. Many bands, though, have to attract audiences on their own. They distribute flyers, send press releases to area newspapers, and send out announcements. Advertising for successful groups is usually handled by a record company or promoter.

Before a performance, musicians arrive early to prepare the stage. They set up instruments and sound systems, check sound quality, and become familiar with the stage and facility. The band reviews the list of songs to be performed and may make changes based on audience responses to previous shows.

Very few pop and rock musicians become successful on their recordings alone. Most perform live and gain a following of fans before they make their first recording.

To be a pop and rock musician, you need to be able to work closely with other artists and to have patience with the rehearsal and recording process. You'll also need persistence to proceed with your ambitions in the face of much rejection.

SCHOOL SUBJECTS
Business, Music
MINIMUM EDUCATION LEVEL
High school diploma
SALARY RANGE
$15,210 to $39,750 to $110,850+
OUTLOOK
About as fast as the average

OTHER ARTICLES TO READ
Audio Recording Engineers
Music Conductors and Directors
Musicians
Music Producers
Singers

Education and Training

It is important to start your music studies as early as possible. While in high school, learn about music theory, the different types of music, how to play one or more instruments, and how to play with other musicians. English composition and creative writing courses will help develop your song writing skills.

A college education is not necessary for becoming a pop and rock musician, but it can help you learn more about music theory and history. You can pursue an education in audio recording, writing, or music at a community college, university, or trade school. A number of seminars, conferences, and workshops are available on song writing, audio recording, and record producing.

Outlook

There will always be thousands more rock and pop musicians than record contracts. But there will also always be opportunities for new performers with record companies and clubs. Record companies are always on the lookout for original sounds and talents. The music industry and the music-buying public have fickle tastes, and often, rock musicians are dropped by their labels when record sales fail to meet expectations.

With recording studios becoming more sophisticated, artists can more effectively promote themselves with quality recordings. Record companies will pay close attention to these independently produced recordings when scouting new talent.

For More Information

To learn more about this career, become involved in your school's various musical groups. Try out for school plays and com-

Pop music icon Madonna entertains thousands during her Re-Invention World Tour. (Landov)

munity theater to get experience performing in front of an audience.

You should also attend musical performances whenever possible. They do not all have to be pop and rock concerts. If you are interested in writing pop and rock music, read the lyrics of your favorite songs, and try to figure out why you like them. Try to write lyrics and put them to music.

American Federation of Musicians of the United States and Canada
1501 Broadway, Suite 600
New York, NY 10036-5501
212-869-1330
http://www.afm.org

American Society of Composers, Authors and Publishers
One Lincoln Plaza
New York, NY 10023-7129
212-621-6000
http://www.ascap.com

Songwriters Guild of America
209 10th Avenue South, Suite 321
Nashville, TN 37203-0743
615-742-9945
corporate@songwritersguild.com
http://www.songwritersguild.com

 # Postal Clerks

SKILLS SPOTLIGHT

What they do

Evaluate and manage information
Help clients and customers
Work with a team

Skills they need

Integrity/honesty
Reading/writing
Responsibility

What Postal Clerks Do

Postal clerks are employees of the United States Postal Service. The equivalent employees at package delivery companies have different titles but perform many of the same duties; at Federal Express they are called *service agents*; at United Parcel Service, they are referred to as *administrative assistants* and *account executives*.

Postal clerks sort mail for delivery and provide service to customers. They work at local post offices or huge central facilities that handle large quantities of mail.

Sorting mail requires identifying letters by ZIP codes and picking out first class, airmail, and special-delivery letters for quick handling. At local post offices, mail that has come from large central facilities is sorted according to specific neighborhoods so that the correct mail carrier can deliver it.

Many of the sorting tasks are now done by machine. Clerks must run these machines and make sure that they operate properly. Clerks also are needed to operate the conveyor belts and loading machines used to transport boxes and packages.

Clerks also handle customer requests. They may sell stamps or provide other services, such as filling out requests for sending a letter by registered mail. These window clerks stand for long periods of time and must answer various customer questions.

In large post offices, clerks may specialize in one task, but in the many small post offices around the country, clerks are asked to do a variety of tasks.

To be a postal clerk, you will need to be able to read quickly and accurately and should have a good memory to remember how to handle each type of letter and package. You also should be able to do the same tasks over and over for long periods of time. Clerks must work closely with other workers, and therefore you should be able to cooperate with others. You also must be able to follow instructions carefully and completely and have a pleasant personality.

SCHOOL SUBJECTS
Mathematics, Speech
MINIMUM EDUCATION LEVEL
High school diploma
SALARY RANGE
$38,980 to $47,890 to $49,750+
OUTLOOK
Decline

OTHER ARTICLES TO READ

Cashiers
Clerks
Counter and Retail Clerks
Mail Carriers
Secretaries

Education and Training

There are no specific educational requirements for postal clerks, but certain classes will be helpful in this position. In high school, take courses in speech, English, computer science, geography, and mathematics.

To apply for this job, you need to be a U.S. citizen or a permanent resident alien and be at least 18 years old or a high school graduate. Applicants must pass a test that measures skills such as the ability to check names and addresses and the ability to memorize how mail is processed. Applicants are also given a physical examination and may be asked to carry mailbags weighing about 70 pounds.

The majority of postal employees are members of the American Postal Workers Union, National Association of Letter Carriers, National Postal Mail Handlers Union, or National Rural Letter Carriers Association.

Outlook

Employment for postal clerks should decline through 2016 because of technologi-

Postal clerks work at the post office to help customers who need to mail packages or do other mail tasks. (Getty Images)

cal developments, including automation and electronic sorting and canceling devices, which allow clerks to handle greater volumes of mail. However, many positions will open as workers retire or move to other occupations.

For More Information

If you are interested in becoming a postal clerk, you can explore this type of work by seeking part-time work during vacations and summer periods, especially the rush holiday periods when many more jobs become available. Related jobs, such as store or office clerk, stock clerk, shipping clerk, or others that require sorting and distributing materials or dealing with the public, might also be beneficial when looking for a position in this area. Also talk to your local post office clerk to get an insider viewpoint.

American Postal Workers Union
1300 L Street NW
Washington, DC 20005
202-842-4200
http://www.apwu.org

National Association of Letter Carriers
100 Indiana Avenue NW
Washington, DC 20001-2144
202-393-4695
nalcinf@nalc.org
http://www.nalc.org

National Postal Mail Handlers Union
1101 Connecticut Avenue NW, Suite 500
Washington, DC 20036-4325
202-833-9095
http://www.npmhu.org

U.S. Postal Service
800-275-8777
http://www.usps.gov

Pottery and Porcelainware Industry Workers

SKILLS SPOTLIGHT

What they do
Evaluate and manage information
Select and apply tools/technology
Work with a team

Skills they need
Creative thinking
Decision making
Speaking/listening

What Pottery and Porcelainware Industry Workers Do

Pottery and porcelainware industry workers make products from clay and other non-metallic minerals. These products include plates and dishes, building materials, bathroom fixtures, dentures, and nose cones for space vehicles. Ceramics is a term used to describe all these products.

The first step in making ceramic products is to crush, grind, clean, and mix clay and other ingredients. The resulting soupy mixture is strained, purified, squeezed, and pressed until it is about as thick as putty. Next, pottery and porcelainware industry workers form the mixture into an object using one of three techniques. Jiggering involves pressing a piece of clay

between two spinning molds. In the casting technique, liquid clay called slip is poured into molds made of plaster of paris. When the clay is dry, the mold is taken apart, and the molded object is removed. Pressing involves firmly packing clay into a container like a mold. Workers who operate pressing machines are called *ram press operators* or *hot press operators*.

After being shaped, objects are dried in a drying room. *Drying machine operators*, or *dryer tenders*, operate controls that adjust the room's temperature and humidity to the proper level for drying of objects.

The final step is to put a glaze finish on the surface of the object. Workers called *dippers* dip each article into the glaze, being careful that the coating is even. Sometimes the glaze is applied by spraying, brushing, or pouring instead of dipping. The article is put in a kiln and baked until the glaze changes into a coating like glass.

The pottery and porcelainware industry employs a wide range of workers. *Ceramic scientists* study ceramic materials and develop new techniques for making these

SCHOOL SUBJECTS
Art, Chemistry, Technical/Shop
MINIMUM EDUCATION LEVEL
High school diploma
SALARY RANGE
$16,100 to $26,480 to $40,370
OUTLOOK
More slowly than the average

OTHER ARTICLES TO READ
Artists
Ceramic Engineers
Coremakers
Glass Manufacturing Workers
Molders

Pottery workers can make their creations by hand, with molds, or by using a potter's wheel. Here, a pottery worker works on a bowl. (forestpath/Shutterstock)

combine classroom instruction with hands-on experience in the workplace.

If you are interested in creating ceramic art, it is common to attend a postsecondary art program with a focus in ceramic art and design. You can choose from specialized art schools (the Art Institute of Chicago and the Maine College of Art, for example) or a number of general universities and colleges. Many students attend these schools to obtain a bachelor of fine arts degree with a major in ceramic art, which traditionally takes four years to finish.

Outlook

The demand for pottery and porcelainware industry workers is expected to grow more slowly than the average through 2016, due in part to increasing factory efficiency and competition from foreign manufacturing plants.

For More Information

Before exploring work opportunities in pottery and porcelainware, explore clay itself, perhaps beginning with a high school ceramics class. Many colleges, universities, community schools, and art schools offer art programs for high school students.

American Ceramic Society
600 N. Cleveland Avenue, Suite 210
Westerville, OH 43082-0921
866-721-3322
customerservice@ceramics.org
http://www.ceramics.org

National Council on Education for the Ceramic Arts
77 Erie Village Square, Suite 280
Erie, CO 80516-6996
866-266-2322
office@nceca.net
http://www.nceca.net

materials. *Ceramic engineers* design, build, and equip factories that make ceramic products. *Ceramic artists* create shapes and decorations for new products. *Ceramic inspectors* grade pieces and reject unacceptable items as they go through the production process. *Warehouse workers* pack items and mark them for shipment.

Education and Training

Pottery and porcelainware workers are usually trained on the job. However, for most positions, employers prefer to hire people who are high school graduates.

Some machine operators and other skilled workers must complete an apprenticeship program that can last up to four years. Apprenticeships are on-the-job training programs that teach workers many of the skills needed in their jobs. They

Power Plant Workers

What they do
Evaluate and manage information
Select and apply tools/technology
Work with a team

Skills they need
Decision making
Reading/writing
Responsibility

What Power Plant Workers Do

Power plant workers control the machinery that generates electricity. Some plants are fueled by coal or nuclear energy that produces steam to drive turbines. Turbines drive generators, which, in turn, produce electric power. Other plants are fueled by falling water; these are called hydroelectric plants.

There are many different types of jobs that power plant workers perform. *Boiler operators*, also called *firers*, work in plants that use steam pressure. These workers keep the boilers going by monitoring the fuel, air, and water supply and maintaining the proper steam pressure. These workers must be able to read and interpret the information shown on control valves, meters, and other instruments.

Turbine operators operate both generators and turbines. These workers record the information from special instruments that show how the turbine or generator is operating and keep the machinery running smoothly. In a large power plant, the turbine operator may have one or more assistants.

Auxiliary equipment operators work with a variety of machines. These include pumps, fans, blowers, compressors, and coal pulverizers. Auxiliary equipment operators monitor this equipment and make small repairs.

Switchboard operators control the flow of electric power through the plant and through the power lines that deliver electricity to the public. They give orders to start and stop generators and connect and disconnect generators to and from power circuits. They often work in control rooms, where they can watch instruments that show what is happening throughout the power plant.

Education and Training

If you are interested in a career as a power plant worker, you will need a high school

SCHOOL SUBJECTS
Mathematics, Technical/Shop
MINIMUM EDUCATION LEVEL
High school diploma
SALARY RANGE
$45,980 to $58,580 to $72,860
OUTLOOK
Decline

OTHER ARTICLES TO READ
Electricians
Electric Power Workers
Industrial Machinery Mechanics
Nuclear Reactor Operators
Stationary Engineers

diploma. Focus on obtaining a solid background in mathematics and science.

Workers on the job are given extensive training that varies in length depending on the job. Training to become an auxiliary equipment operator usually lasts from one to three years. Training to become a boiler, turbine, or switchboard operator can take from four to eight years. In nuclear power plants, trainees for operator positions need a strong background in science and mathematics and, preferably, a college degree.

Power plants that generate electricity using nuclear reactors are regulated by the Nuclear Regulatory Commission (NRC). Operators in nuclear plants must be licensed by the NRC because only NRC-licensed operators are authorized to control any equipment in the plant that affects the operation of the nuclear reactor. Nuclear reactor operators are also required to undertake regular drug testing.

Many workers in power plants are members of either the International Brotherhood of Electrical Workers or the Utility Workers Union of America. Union members traditionally have been paid better than nonunion members.

A power plant worker monitors the equipment and workings of the power plant. (Philippe Psaila/Photo Researchers, Inc.)

Outlook

Consumer demand for electric power is expected to increase in the next decade, but power-generating plants will install more automatic control systems and more efficient equipment, which will result in declining job opportunities through 2016.

Most job openings will develop when experienced workers retire or leave to go into other occupations. Those skilled in computers and working with automated equipment will have the best employment prospects.

For More Information

There is little opportunity for part-time or summer work experience in this field. However, many power plants (both nuclear and nonnuclear) have visitor centers where you can observe some of the power plant operations and learn about the various processes for converting energy into electricity. You might also find information on this field at libraries, or on the Internet.

American Public Power Association
1875 Connecticut Avenue, NW, Suite 1200
Washington, DC 20009-5715
202-467-2900
mrufe@appanet.org
http://www.appanet.org

International Brotherhood of Electrical Workers
900 Seventh Street, NW
Washington, DC 20001-3886
202-833-7000
http://www.ibew.org/contact.htm
http://www.ibew.org

Utility Workers Union of America
815 16th Street, NW
Washington, DC 20006-4101
202-974-8200
http://www.uwua.net

Precision Machinists and Metalworkers

SKILLS SPOTLIGHT
What they do
Help clients and customers
Select and apply tools/technology
Work with a team

Skills they need
Mathematics
Reading/writing
Reasoning

What Precision Machinists and Metalworkers Do

Precision machinists and metalworkers use machine tools to produce precision metal parts. Machine tools can be used to cut, drill, bore, turn, mill, plan, and grind.

After receiving a job assignment, precision machinists and metalworkers first read blueprints and written directions. Next, they plan and select the proper tools and materials and mark the metal for places to cut. Then they set up the machine and its controls, position the metal piece, and make the necessary cuts. The machine tool is constantly monitored during operation, and when necessary, the precision machinist or metalworker adds coolants or lubricants to ensure that the machine runs smoothly. After the shaping is completed,

machinists and metalworkers sometimes finish the metal piece by hand, using files and scrapers. Finally, the finished parts are assembled with hand tools.

In the past, machinists and metalworkers have had direct control of their machines. However, the increased use of computer-controlled machines has changed the nature of the work. Now, machinists and metalworkers often work with tool programmers to set up their machines, or they may learn how to program the machine tools themselves.

Most machinists and metalworkers work in small machining shops or for manufacturing companies that produce goods, such as industrial machinery, cars, trucks, and airplanes. *Maintenance machinists*, however, work in any industry that uses production machinery.

To be a successful precision machinist and metalworker, you must have mathematics skills and be able to understand and visualize spatial relationships in order to read and interpret engineering drawings. You should also have excellent manual

SCHOOL SUBJECTS
Computer science, Technical/Shop
MINIMUM EDUCATION LEVEL
Apprenticeship
SALARY RANGE
$23,350 to $32,550 to $46,800
OUTLOOK
More slowly than the average

OTHER ARTICLES TO READ
Fluid Power Technicians
Heat Treaters
Layout Workers
Sheet Metal Workers
Welders and Welding Technicians

Fast Fact

There are approximately 397,000 precision machinists working in the United States as of 2006, the latest year for which figures are available.

dexterity, good vision and hand-eye coordination, and the concentration necessary to do highly accurate work.

Education and Training

For trainee or apprentice jobs, most companies prefer to hire high school or vocational school graduates. Recommended courses in high school include algebra, geometry, mechanical drawing, blueprint reading, machine shop, and computer science. Classes in electronics and hydraulics also are helpful.

To work as a machinist or metalworker, you must complete either an apprenticeship or an on-the-job training program. Apprenticeships, which most employers prefer, generally consist of four to five years of carefully planned activities, including shop training and related classroom instruction.

You can also enter the field directly from high school or vocational school and receive on-the-job training. In this case, newly hired workers train with various machines while being supervised by experienced machinists or metalworkers. Trainees usually begin as machine operators.

Then, as they show the necessary aptitude, they are given additional training on the machines they are operating.

Outlook

Employment growth for precision machinists and metalworkers is expected to be slower than the average for all occupations through 2016. Automation is contributing to this slower growth rate. Even so, many openings will arise from the need to replace machinists who retire or transfer to other jobs. In recent years, employers have reported difficulty in attracting skilled workers to machining occupations.

For More Information

To observe precision machinists and metalworkers at work, ask a school counselor or teacher to arrange a field trip to a machine shop.

International Association of Machinists and Aerospace Workers
9000 Machinists Place
Upper Marlboro, MD 20772-2687
301-967-4500
websteward@iamaw.org
http://www.iamaw.org

National Tooling & Machining Association
9300 Livingston Road
Fort Washington, MD 20744-4914
800-248-6862
info@ntma.org
http://www.ntma.org

Precision Machined Products Association
6700 West Snowville Road
Brecksville, OH 44141-3292
440-526-0300
webmaster@pmpa.org
http://www.pmpa.org

Prepress Workers

SKILLS SPOTLIGHT

What they do
Communicate ideas
Select and apply tools/technology
Work with a team

Skills they need
Reading/writing
Social
Speaking/listening

What Prepress Workers Do

Prepress workers arrange and prepare the text and pictures that eventually become newspapers, magazines, books, and other printed materials. They work in commercial printing, business printing, newspaper printing, and printing trade service firms.

A variety of prepress careers are available. Some are skilled crafts that take years to master, but most prepress work now is computer based and requires a high degree of computer literacy.

Compositors and typesetters set and arrange type for printing, either by hand or electronically (such as phototypesetting). *Paste-up workers* position illustrations and lay out columns of type.

Manual prepress work is being eliminated by *desktop publishing specialists*, who typeset, layout, and design text and graphics on a personal computer. Camera-ready photos and art are scanned by the *scanner operator*, converting them into electronic images that can be integrated into a file.

Electronic files are reviewed by *pre-flight technicians* to ensure that all the elements are properly formatted and set up.

Once the final version of a page has been assembled, a photographic negative of the page is made. Most often, film negatives are now produced directly from the computer. If not, or if camera-ready art is involved, a *camera operator* photographs the material and develops a negative.

It is the job of the *film stripper* to make any last-minute changes and assemble the different pieces of film into position. The *platemaker*, often called a *lithographer*, then makes the printing plate from the film negative. The plate is what goes into the printing press.

Prepress work requires strong communication skills, attention to detail, and the ability to perform well in a high-pressure, deadline-driven environment. Physically, you should have good manual dexterity, good eyesight, and overall visual perception. Artistic skill is an advantage in nearly any prepress job.

SCHOOL SUBJECTS
Computer science, Technical/Shop
MINIMUM EDUCATION LEVEL
High school diploma
SALARY RANGE
$17,050 to $33,570 to $58,450
OUTLOOK
Decline

OTHER ARTICLES TO READ
Art Directors
Book Editors
Desktop Publishing Specialists
Graphic Designers
Graphics Programmers
Printing Press Operators

Fast Fact

There are more than 47,000 printing plants in the United States.

Education and Training

Educational requirements for prepress workers vary by duty, but most prepress jobs require at least a high school diploma. Recommended high school courses include English, computer science, mathematics, photography, chemistry, physics, drawing, and art.

The more traditional jobs, such as camera operator, film stripper, lithographic artist, and platemaker, require longer, more specialized preparation. This might involve an apprenticeship or a two-year associate's degree. But these jobs now are on the decline, as they are being replaced by computerized processes.

Postsecondary education is strongly encouraged for most prepress positions and is a requirement for some jobs, including any managerial role.

Outlook

Overall employment in the prepress portion of the printing industry is expected to decline through 2016. While it is anticipated that the demand for printed materials will increase, the demand for prepress work will not, mainly because of new technologies. Employment growth for desktop publishing specialists, however, is expected to be much faster than the average. And specialized computer skills will increasingly be needed to handle direct-to-plate and other new technology.

For More Information

A summer job or internship doing basic word processing or desktop publishing is beneficial.

Association for Suppliers of Printing, Publishing and Converting Technologies
Education Committee
1899 Preston White Drive
Reston, VA 20191-4367
703-264-7200
npes@npes.org
http://www.npes.org/education/index.html

Graphic Arts Information Network
Graphic Arts Technical Foundation/Printing Industries of America
200 Deer Run Road
Sewickley, PA 15143-2324
800-910-4283
gain@piagatf.org
http://www.gain.net

Graphic Communications Conference of the International Brotherhood of Teamsters
1900 L Street NW
Washington, DC 20036-5002
202-462-1400
http://www.gciu.org/abouthed.shtml

NAPL—National Association for Printing Leadership
75 West Century Road, Suite 100
Paramus, NJ 07652-1408
800-642-6275
http://www.napl.org

Preschool Teachers

SKILLS SPOTLIGHT
What they do
Communicate ideas
Work with a team
Teach

Skills they need
Creative thinking
Reading/writing
Speaking/listening

What Preschool Teachers Do

Preschool teachers teach children who are between two and five years old. They work in child care centers, nursery schools, Head Start programs, and other private and public programs. They prepare children for kindergarten and grade school by teaching letters, numbers, colors, days of the week, and how to tell time. Preschool teachers also introduce children to books, educational games, and computer software. These teachers show their young students social skills through play and activities. Their work differs from kindergarten teachers, who focus more on numbers, words, and writing skills.

In preschool classrooms, teachers plan and lead activities such as storytelling, arts and crafts projects, and singing, depending on the abilities and interests of the children. Teachers have to think about which skills children should be learning at a particular age. They encourage the children to think creatively and to express their feelings and ideas. They help them develop social skills as they get used to being in school with other children and introduce them to the concepts of sharing and playing in groups. Other social skills might include manners, hygiene, and how to clean up after themselves.

Preschool teachers also get to know the children's parents and regularly provide them with reports on progress and behavior. They might also invite parents along on field trips and to the classroom to observe.

Because young children look up to adults and learn through example, it is especially important that a preschool teacher be a good role model.

Education and Training

While in high school, you should take child development, home economics, and other classes that involve you with child care. You'll also need a fundamental understanding of the general subjects you will be

SCHOOL SUBJECTS
Art, English

MINIMUM EDUCATION LEVEL
Some postsecondary training

SALARY RANGE
$16,490 to $25,300 to $45,770

OUTLOOK
About as fast as the average

OTHER ARTICLES TO READ
Child Care Workers
Elementary School Teachers
School Administrators
Special Education Teachers
Teacher Aides

Preschool teachers help their students learn skills that they will need when they enter elementary school. (Matka Wariatka/Shutterstock)

introducing to preschool students, so take English, science, and math.

Large child care centers sometimes hire high school graduates who have some child care experience and give them on-the-job training. For example, the American Montessori Society offers a career program that requires a three-month training period followed by a year of supervised on-the-job training.

Some schools require preschool teachers to have bachelor's degrees. Many colleges and universities offer programs in early childhood education and child care. In some states, preschool teachers are required to be licensed. The Child Development Associate credential qualifies preschool teachers in some states. Unlike preschool teachers, kindergarten teachers must have education degrees and state certification.

Outlook

Employment opportunities for preschool teachers are expected to increase about as fast as the average for all occupations through 2016. Specific job opportunities vary from state to state and depend on demographic characteristics and level of government funding. Jobs should be available at private child care centers, nursery schools, Head Start facilities, public and private kindergartens, and laboratory schools connected with universities and colleges.

For More Information

There are many volunteer opportunities for working with young children. Check with your library or local literacy program about tutoring children and reading to preschoolers. Summer day camps or church schools with preschool classes may offer assistant or aide opportunities.

American Montessori Society
281 Park Avenue South
New York, NY 10010-6102
212-358-1250
ams@amshq.org
http://www.amshq.org

National Association for the Education of Young Children
1313 L Street, NW, Suite 500
Washington, DC 20005-4110
800-424-2460
webmaster@naeyc.org
http://www.naeyc.org

National Association of Child Care Professionals
PO Box 90723
Austin, TX 78709-0723
800-537-1118
admin@naccp.org
http://www.naccp.org

Press Secretaries

What Press Secretaries Do

Press secretaries are media representatives who help politicians promote themselves and their issues to voters. Once elected to office, politicians need press secretaries to answer the questions of journalists, prepare speeches, and organize press conferences. These media representatives also work for corporations and for organizations and nonprofit groups advocating for legislative issues.

Press secretaries serve on the congressional staffs of senators and representatives, or in the office of the president. Press secretaries write media releases and opinion pieces to publicize the efforts of the government officials for whom they work. They also schedule press conferences and prepare their employers for interviews.

These workers are often called *spin doctors* because of their ability to manipulate the press, possibly putting a good spin on a news story that best suits the purposes of their clients. Using newspapers and radio and TV broadcasts, press secretaries may attempt to downplay public relations disasters. During very sensitive times, such as during scandals or foreign conflicts, or after unpopular political decisions, press secretaries must answer questions selectively and carefully. They may be responsible for bringing public attention to important issues and may help develop support for school funding, environmental concerns, and other community needs.

To be a press secretary, you need to be very organized and capable of juggling many different tasks, from quickly writing ads and press releases to developing budgets and expense accounts. You need good problem-solving skills and some imagination when putting a positive spin on negative issues.

Education and Training

In high school, English composition, drama, and speech classes will help you develop

SCHOOL SUBJECTS
Government, Journalism

MINIMUM EDUCATION LEVEL
Bachelor's degree

SALARY RANGE
$44,870 to $56,910 to $121,500

OUTLOOK
Faster than the average

OTHER ARTICLES TO READ
Ambassadors
Appointed and Elected Officials
Campaign Workers
Congressional Aides
Lobbyists
Political Scientists
Public Relations Specialists

good communication skills, while government, history, and civics classes will teach you about the structure of government.

Most press secretaries have bachelor's degrees, and some also hold master's degrees, doctorates, and law degrees. Enroll in a four-year college, and pursue a well-rounded education; press secretaries need a good understanding of the history and culture of the United States and foreign countries. Some of the majors you should consider as an undergraduate are journalism, political science, English, marketing, and economics. You might then choose to pursue a graduate degree in journalism, political science, public administration, or international relations.

You should pursue an internship with a local or state official or your congressional member in the Senate or House of Representatives. Another option is to pursue a journalism internship with a local or national publication or the news department of a radio or TV station.

Robert Gibbs, Barack Obama's press secretary, handles questions from reporters. (Associated Press)

Outlook

Employment growth for press secretaries is expected to be faster than the average through 2016. Press secretaries will take on additional duties as more news networks and news magazines closely follow the decisions and actions of government officials.

The Pew Research Center, which surveys public opinion on political issues, has found that most Americans are concerned about negative campaigning done by political consultants. In the future, negative campaigning may be affected somewhat by developing technology. Voters are now able to access more information about candidates and issues via the Internet. Also, the increase in the number of channels available to cable TV watchers makes it

more difficult for candidates to advertise to a general audience.

For More Information

Get involved with your school government as well as with committees and clubs that have officers and elections. You can also become involved in local, state, and federal elections by volunteering for campaigns.

American Association of Political Consultants
600 Pennsylvania Avenue, SE, Suite 330
Washington, DC 20003-6300
202-544-9815
http://www.theaapc.org

The Pew Research Center for the People & the Press
1615 L Street NW, Suite 700
Washington, DC 20036-5621
202-419-4350
http://www.people-press.org

Printing Press Operators

What Printing Press Operators Do

Today's printing presses are much faster than they used to be, and most are controlled by computers. Some presses can print nearly 150,000 newspapers an hour. Running these fast, modern presses is the job of *printing press operators* and their assistants.

These workers set up, operate, clean, and maintain presses. The web press is the most common press used for printing newspapers, magazines, and books. With a web press, the ink is on a revolving cylinder that prints onto a continuous sheet of paper (the web) coming off a giant roll. The other type of press is a sheet-fed press, which prints on single sheets of paper rather than on a continuous roll.

Press operators first prepare the press. They inspect and oil the moving parts and clean and adjust the ink rollers and ink fountains. When they receive the printing plates from the prepress area, they mount them into place on the printing surface or cylinder. They mix and match the ink, fill the ink fountains, and adjust the ink flow and dampening systems. They also load the paper, adjust the press to the paper size, feed the paper through the cylinders and, on a web press, adjust the tension controls. When this is done, a proof sheet is run off for the customer's review.

When the proof has been approved and final adjustments have been made, the press run begins. During the run, press operators constantly check the quality of the printed sheets and make any necessary adjustments. They make sure the print is clear and properly positioned and that ink is not blotting onto other sheets. If the job involves color, they make sure that the colors line up properly. Operators also monitor the chemical properties of the ink and correct temperatures in the drying chamber, if the press has one. On a web press, the feeding and tension mechanisms must be continually monitored. If the paper tears or jams, it must be rethreaded. As a roll of paper runs out, a new one must be spliced onto the old one.

SCHOOL SUBJECTS
Mathematics, Technical/Shop

MINIMUM EDUCATION LEVEL
High school diploma

SALARY RANGE
$20,750 to $37,880 to $59,990

OUTLOOK
More slowly than the average

OTHER ARTICLES TO READ
General Maintenance Mechanics
Industrial Machinery Mechanics
Packaging Machinery Technicians
Prepress Workers

A printing press operator checks a page for quality during the printing process. (Rubberball Productions)

When the press run is finished, the press operators clean and check the press so that it is ready for another printing job.

Strong communication skills, both verbal and written, are a must for press operators and assistants. They also must be able to work well as a team, both with each other and with others in the printing company. Working well under pressure is another requirement because most print jobs run on tight deadlines.

Education and Training

A high school diploma is the minimum education required for a position as a printing press operator. Classes in art, print shop, mathematics, chemistry, physics, and computer science are helpful. Computer training is essential for anyone entering the field. An apprenticeship or postsecondary training in a vocational-technical or graphic arts program is strongly recommended.

Outlook

Employment growth for press operators is expected to be slower than the average through 2016. The larger, more efficient machines in use today are able to handle the increased demand for printed materials, such as advertising, direct mail pieces, computer software packaging, books, and magazines.

Newcomers to the field are likely to encounter stiff competition from experienced workers or workers who have completed retraining programs to update their skills. Opportunities are expected to be greatest for people who have completed formal apprenticeships or postsecondary training programs.

For More Information

Some schools offer print shop classes, which provide the most direct exposure to this work. Work on your school newspaper or yearbook to learn more about the printing process.

Association for Suppliers of Printing, Publishing and Converting Technologies
Education Committee
1899 Preston White Drive
Reston, VA 20191-4367
703-264-7200
npes@npes.org
http://www.npes.org/education/index.html

Graphic Arts Information Network
Graphic Arts Technical Foundation/Printing
Industries of America
200 Deer Run Road
Sewickley, PA 15143-2324
800-910-4283
gain@piagatf.org
http://www.gain.net

National Council for Skill Standards in Graphic Communication
800 Main Street, Building Q
Pewaukee, WI 53072-4601
262-695-6252
maspenson@piw.org
http://www.ncssgc.org

Private Investigators

SKILLS SPOTLIGHT

What they do
Evaluate and manage ideas
Exercise leadership
Help clients and customers

Skills they need
Integrity/honesty
Reading/writing
Speaking/listening

What Private Investigators Do

Private investigators, or *private detectives*, investigate crimes, help find missing persons, serve as bodyguards to important people, and collect information for trials and other legal proceedings. They spend much of their time in library research, fact checking, and interviews.

Private investigators do many of the same things as police officers. They gather clues from accidents, observe suspects, and check people's personal histories to learn more about their backgrounds. There are two important differences between police officers and investigators: investigators do not have to follow the same legal procedures when they interview suspects and collect evidence, and investigators cannot make arrests. Private detectives sometimes work with police officers to solve crimes.

Private investigators usually work for agencies. Clients come to these agencies with specific problems. For example, a business owner might hire an investigator to prevent shoplifting, vandalism, or another type of business crime. Investigators may be asked to look into insurance claims to make sure that people who are claiming property damage have actually had property destroyed or stolen. They may be hired to find a missing person, gather information on the background of persons involved in divorce or child custody cases, administer lie detection tests, debug offices and telephones, or offer security services. They use cameras, video equipment, tape recorders, and lock picks in compliance with legal restrictions to obtain necessary information. They conduct interviews with anyone who might be involved in a case, including family, friends, neighbors, employers, and coworkers.

In all cases, investigators report to their clients on the details of their case. These reports are usually written and then explained orally.

SCHOOL SUBJECTS
English, Government, History

MINIMUM EDUCATION LEVEL
High school diploma

SALARY RANGE
$20,990 to $37,640 to $72,280

OUTLOOK
Faster than the average

OTHER ARTICLES TO READ
Crime Analysts
Deputy U.S. Marshals
Detectives
FBI Agents
Forensic Experts
Police Officers
Spies

Growth Field

Between 2006 and 2016 the number of private detectives is expected to grow from 52,000 to 61,000, an increase of about 18 percent.

A private investigator's work can lead to the recovery of stolen valuables, the arrest of a criminal, or the uncovering of a spy operation. But for every success there are many hours of searching for clues. Investigations can be dangerous. Investigators may have to go into rough neighborhoods late at night looking for witnesses, or they may be threatened by suspects. Most of the work, however, is safe.

Education and Training

Many people become investigators after working as police officers. There are several detective training programs that show you how to locate missing persons, interview people, check public records, lift fingerprints, pick locks, and operate cameras and other surveillance equipment. These programs usually are several months long. You then receive on-the-job training at a detective agency before you become an investigator. Most programs accept only high school graduates. There are also many community colleges and universities that have degree programs in criminal justice or a related field.

Most states require private investigators to take a licensing test. Those who carry a gun usually have to pass an examination to show they know how to use a firearm.

Outlook

Employment growth for private investigators is also predicted to be faster than the average through 2016. It is important to keep in mind that law enforcement or comparable experience is often required for employment. The use of private investigators by insurance firms, restaurants, hotels, and other businesses is on the rise. An area of particular growth is the investigation of the various forms of computer fraud.

For More Information

Practice your detective skills by playing board games and computer games that test your mystery- and puzzle-solving skills. Ask your librarian to help you find books, both fiction and nonfiction, on detective work and crime solving.

National Association of Investigative Specialists
PO Box 82148
Austin, TX 78708-2148
512-719-3595
http://www.pimall.com/nais

U.S. Department of Justice
Drug Enforcement Administration
Office of Personnel
8701 Morrissette Drive
Springfield, VA 22152-1080
800-332-4288
http://www.usdoj.gov/dea

Process Servers

What Process Servers Do

Process servers are licensed by the courts to serve legal papers, such as summonses, subpoenas, and court orders, to people involved in legal disputes. People served may include witnesses, defendants in lawsuits, or the employers of workers whose wages are being garnished by court order.

Process servers are responsible for notifying people in a timely and legal fashion that they are required to appear in court. They work for attorneys, government agencies (such as a state's attorney general's office), or any person who files a lawsuit, seeks a divorce, or begins a legal action.

A process server is involved only in civil matters. Criminal arrest warrants or papers ordering the seizure of property are served exclusively by sheriffs, constables, and other law enforcement officials. Process servers know the rules of civil procedure, such as expiration dates of court documents. Subpoenas, eviction notices, notices of trustee sales, writs of garnishment (order to bring property to the court), summonses, and court orders each must be served according to complicated regulations. The process server is responsible for making sure that every service is valid by following these rules and exceptions.

Much of a process server's time is spent skip-tracing—that is, trying to locate a person who has moved or who may be avoiding service. Process servers sometimes have to search for a last known address, a place of business, or even a photograph of the person. They question neighbors or co-workers and use public information provided by government offices (such as the assessor's office), voter registration, or the court clerk to locate the person.

Because process serving is a face-to-face job, people who excel in this field are usually bold, confident, and skilled at working with people. Gaining a reputation as reliable and responsible will go a long way with prospective clients who want someone who will not give up on serving papers to

---

SCHOOL SUBJECTS
English, Government

MINIMUM EDUCATION LEVEL
High school diploma

SALARY RANGE
$22,800 to $34,730 to $76,020

OUTLOOK
About as fast as the average

OTHER ARTICLES TO READ
Bounty Hunters
Detectives
Lawyers
Legal Secretaries
Paralegals
Police Officers

Fast Fact

The term *process server* was coined in the 1930s to describe an official who could serve legal documents but who had no other law enforcement powers.

people. Because process servers often serve papers to people who do not want them, a certain element of danger is involved. Process servers must be willing to take that risk in some situations.

Education and Training

To prepare for a career as a process server, take courses in English, political science, communication, and any law or business-related subjects. Training in a foreign language can also be extremely helpful because process servers may encounter non-English speakers.

Although college is not required, advanced courses in psychology, communications, business, and legal studies are beneficial to process servers. The Process Server Institute holds training seminars focused on process serving.

According to the National Association of Investigation Specialists, any U.S. citizen who is not personally involved in the case, is over the age of 18, and who resides in the state where the matter is to be tried may be a process server for a specific legal matter. However, people who serve papers on a regular basis usually must register with their particular state. It is recommended that process servers obtain

private detective status with their particular state. You can get more information from your local office of the Clerk of the Superior Court.

Outlook

Employment opportunities for process servers will grow as the number of civil lawsuits increases. A single legal case can produce anywhere from one service to dozens, when taking into account subpoenas, supporting orders, writs of garnishment, and other documents.

Some sheriff's departments are now beginning to rely solely on private process servers, since they cannot effectively compete with the faster and more inexpensive private process-serving companies.

For More Information

Since most court records are public, you could look at actual files of court cases to become familiar with the types of papers served and examine affidavits filed by process servers.

National Association of Professional Process Servers
PO Box 4547
Portland, OR 97208-4547
800-477-8211
administrator@napps.org
http://www.napps.com

Process Server Institute
667 Folsom Street, 2nd Floor
San Francisco, CA 94107-1314
415-495-3850
http://www.psinstitute.com

United States Process Servers Association
PO Box 19767
St. Louis, MO 63144-0167
866-367-2841
http://www.usprocessservers.com

Production Assistants

What Production Assistants Do

Production assistants (PAs) perform a variety of tasks for film, television, and video producers and other staff members. Production assistants' duties range from making sure the star has coffee in the morning to stopping street traffic so a director can film a scene. They photocopy the script for actors, help set up equipment, and perform other tasks. The best PAs know where to be at the right time to make themselves useful.

Some production assistants are responsible for keeping production files in order. These files include contracts, budgets, page changes (old pages from a script that have been revised), and other records. The documents must be kept organized and accessible for whenever the producer may need them.

Production assistants may also have to keep the producer's production folder in order and up to date. PAs make sure the folder includes the shooting schedule, the most recent version of the budget, cast and crew lists with phone numbers, a phone sheet detailing all production-related phone calls the producer needs to make, and the up-to-date shooting script. As new versions of these forms are created, PAs update the producer's folder and file the older versions for reference.

PAs schedule an hour or so in a producer's schedule to watch the dailies (the film shot each day) and make related calls to discuss them with other staff members. PAs make travel reservations, arrange hotel accommodations, and arrange for rehearsal space. They run errands and communicate messages for producers, directors, actors, musicians, and other members of the technical crew.

PAs who work in television studios for live shows, such as news programs and talk shows, record news feeds, answer phones, operate teleprompters, coordinate tapes, and assist editors. They assist with booking guests and arranging interviews.

SCHOOL SUBJECTS
Business, Theater/Dance
MINIMUM EDUCATION LEVEL
High school diploma
SALARY RANGE
$17,840 to $30,800 to $51,040
OUTLOOK
About as fast as the average

OTHER ARTICLES TO READ
Actors
Artists
Cinematographers
Film and Television Directors
Film and Television Editors
Film and Television Producers

Education and Training

Take courses in photography, film, broadcast journalism, and media to learn about the film and television industries.

There are no formal education requirements for production assistants. Most people in the industry consider the position a stepping stone into other careers in the industry. You learn much of what you will need to know on the set of a film, following the instructions of crew members and other assistants. Many film students work part time or on a contract basis as production assistants to gain experience while they are still in school.

Outlook

There will always be a need for assistants in film and television production. However, competition for jobs can be tough, since it is such a good entry-level position for someone who wants to make connections and learn about the industry. Typically, production assistants usually do not stay in their jobs more than one or two years, so turnover is fairly high. PAs will find employment anywhere a motion picture, television show, or video is being filmed, but more opportunities exist in Los Angeles and New York City. There may be opportunities at local television stations or smaller production companies that produce educational and corporate videos.

For More Information

Join a film club at your school or community center. Theater experience can be helpful, and you may be able to find volunteer opportunities at a local theater or on

Fast Fact

Production assistants should pick up industry lingo while on the job. A *call sheet* is a list of the actors needed for each scene to be filmed that day. A *hot set* is a set on which filming is currently taking place. Most important, *craft service* is the snack and food provider for a production.

a low-budget film project. Read about the film and television industries in such publications as *Daily Variety* (http://www.variety.com), *Hollywood Reporter* (http://www.hollywoodreporter.com), and *The Rundown* (http://www.tvrundown.com).

American Film Institute
2021 North Western Avenue
Los Angeles, CA 90027-1657
323-856-7600
http://www.afi.com

American Society of Cinematographers
PO Box 2230
Hollywood, CA 90078-2230
800-448-0145
office@theasc.com
http://www.theasc.com

National Association of Broadcasters
1771 N Street, NW
Washington, DC 20036-2800
202-429-5300
nab@nab.org
http://www.nab.org

Professional Athletes— Extreme Sports

What Professional Athletes— Extreme Sports Do

Professional athletes—extreme sports are characterized as people who enjoy living life on the edge. Their playing arena includes many uncontrollable environmental forces such as weather and terrain that impact the outcome of their competitions.

The list of extreme sports has changed during the past 20 years, as evidenced by the events included in the current X Games, the premier showcase for these sports. Among the sports featured in the most recent X Games are rallying (motor competition on private or public roads) and snowskating (a crossover sport for inline skaters on ski slopes).

Like traditional professional athletes, extreme players spend a great deal of time honing their sport skills. And while the challenges for traditional sports players are very demanding, those for extreme athletes are filled with even greater physical and mental pressure. Extreme sports are accentuated by high speeds, radical heights, and unprecedented physical endurance and exertion.

Most extreme sports involve special gear and equipment for stunt performances. Many professional extreme athletes earn money through product endorsements. For example, a BMX rider, may wear a particular manufacturer's helmet and, in exchange, the helmet manufacturer provides a financial incentive to the athlete for displaying the product during tournaments and competitions.

Education and Training

In high school, concentrate on physical education courses to sharpen your athletic abilities. In addition, take biology to understand how your body works and health

SCHOOL SUBJECTS
Biology, Health, Physical education
MINIMUM EDUCATION LEVEL
High school diploma
SALARY RANGE
$15,110 to $38,520 to $100,410+
OUTLOOK
About as fast as the average

OTHER ARTICLES TO READ
Athletic Directors
Physical Education Teachers
Professional Athletes—Individual Sports
Sports Agents
Sports Coaches
Sports Scouts

and nutrition courses to understand how to maintain and take care of it.

There are no formal education requirements for extreme sports athletes. Becoming a professional athlete is the result of years of training and dedication to the sport. Extreme athletes usually begin by participating in noncompetitive events and then, as they hone their skills, advance to competitive tournaments.

Since many professional athletes—especially extreme athletes—retire at young ages, those with college business, management, and marketing degrees can position themselves for sports-related careers long after their performance days have passed.

Outlook

As with traditional professional athletes, the outlook for those in the extreme field will vary by the popularity and the number of athletes currently competing in the sport. Overall, the extreme sports field is expected to grow about as fast as the average. The popularity of extreme sports, heightened by the marketing efforts of the X Games' sponsors and product endorsements, does not appear to be diminishing.

For More Information

If you are interested in pursuing a career in professional sports as an extreme athlete, you should start participating in that sport as much and as early as possible. Be aware, however, that many of these sports are not recommended for young people because of the dangers associated with them. When participating in any sport, be sure to use

Extreme sports athletes, such as snowboarders, receive sponsorships from companies, which enable them to make their sport a career. (Eric Limon/Shutterstock)

the appropriate gear and equipment and practice correct safety measures.

Amateur Athletic Union
1910 Hotel Plaza Boulevard
Lake Buena Vista, FL 32830-2409
407-934-7200
http://www.aausports.org

Sporting Goods Manufacturers Association
1150 17th Street, NW, Suite 850
Washington DC 20036-4603
202-775-1762
info@sgma.com
http://www.sgma.com

Professional Athletes— Individual Sports

What Professional Athletes— Individual Sports Do

In contrast with amateur athletes who play or compete in amateur circles for titles or trophies only, *professional athletes* participate in individual sports such as tennis, figure-skating, golf, running, or boxing, competing against others to win prizes and money.

Depending on the nature of the specific sport, most athletes compete against a field of individual competitors that can be as small as one person or as large as the number of qualified competitors, anywhere from six to 30 or more. Within a professional sport there are usually different levels of competition based on age, ability, and gender.

In addition to stretching and exercising the specific muscles used in any given sport, athletes concentrate on developing excellent eating and sleeping habits that will help them remain in top condition throughout the year. Although certain sports have a particular season, most professional athletes train all year on their own or with a coach, friend, parent, or trainer. Often, an athlete's training focuses less on the overall game or program in which the athlete participates, than on specific areas or details of that game or program. Figure skaters, for example, will not simply keep going through their entire long programs from start to finish but instead will focus on the jumps, turns, and hand movements that refine the program. Similarly, sprinters do not keep running only the sprint distances they race in during a meet; instead, they vary their workouts to include some distance work, some sprints, a lot of weight training to build strength, and maybe some mental exercises to build control and focus while in the starter's blocks. Tennis players routinely spend hours just practicing their forehand, down-the-line shots.

SCHOOL SUBJECTS
Health, Physical education

MINIMUM EDUCATION LEVEL
High school diploma

SALARY RANGE
$15,110 to $38,520 to $100,410+

OUTLOOK
About as fast as the average

OTHER ARTICLES TO READ
Athletic Directors
Physical Education Teachers
Professional Athletes—Team Sports
Sports Agents
Sports Coaches
Sports Scouts

United States speed skating champion and gold medalist Bonnie Blair races on the ice. (Vandystadt/Photo Researchers, Inc.)

Athletes often watch videotapes or films of their previous practices or competitions to see where they can improve their performance. They also study what the other competitors are doing to prepare strategies for winning. Diligence, perseverance, hard work, ambition, and courage are all essential qualities for someone who dreams of making a career as a professional athlete.

Education and Training

A high school diploma will provide the basic skills that you will need in your long climb to becoming a professional athlete. Business and mathematics classes will teach you how to manage money wisely. Speech classes will help you become a better communicator. Physical education classes will help you build your strength, agility, and competitive spirit. You should also participate in every organized sport that your school offers and that interests you.

There are no formal education requirements for sports, although certain competitions and training opportunities are only available to those enrolled in four-year colleges and universities. Collegiate-level competitions are where most athletes in some sports like tennis and golf improve their skills.

Outlook

The outlook for professional athletes will vary depending on the sport, its popularity, and the number of athletes currently competing. Overall, employment opportunities are expected to grow about as fast as the average through 2016. Some sports, however, may experience an increase in popularity, which will translate into greater opportunities for higher salaries, prize monies, and commercial endorsements.

For More Information

If you are interested in pursuing a career in professional sports, you should start participating in that sport as much and as early as possible. By playing the sport and by talking to coaches, trainers, and athletes in the field, you can decide whether you like the sport enough to make it a career, determine if you have enough talent, and gain new insight into the field. You can also contact professional organizations and associations for information on how to best prepare for a career in their sport.

Amateur Athletic Union
1910 Hotel Plaza Boulevard
Lake Buena Vista, FL 32830-2409
407-934-7200
http://www.aausports.org

American Alliance for Health, Physical Education, Recreation, and Dance
1900 Association Drive
Reston, VA 20191-1598
800-213-7193
info@aahperd.org
http://www.aahperd.org

Professional Athletes— Team Sports

What Professional Athletes— Team Sports Do

Professional athletic teams compete against one another to win titles, championships, and series; team members are paid salaries and bonuses for their work, unlike amateur athletes who play or compete in amateur circles for titles or trophies only. Team sports include football, basketball, hockey, baseball, and soccer.

Competitions are organized by local, regional, national, and international organizations and associations whose primary functions are to promote the sport and sponsor competitive events.

Professional teams train for most of the year, but unlike athletes in individual sports, athletes who are members of a team usually have more of an off-season. The training programs of professional athletes differ according to the season. Follow-ing an off-season, most team sports have a training season, in which they begin to focus their workouts after a period of relative inactivity to develop or maintain strength, cardiovascular ability, flexibility, endurance, speed, and quickness, as well as to focus on technique and control. During the season, the team coach, physician, trainers, and physical therapists organize specific routines, programs, or exercises to target game skills as well as individual athletic weaknesses.

In addition to stretching and exercising the specific muscles used in any given sport, athletes concentrate on developing excellent eating and sleeping habits that will help them remain in top condition throughout the year.

The coaching or training staff often films the games and practices so that the team can benefit from watching their individual performances, as well as their combined play. By watching their performances, team members can learn how to improve their techniques and strategies. It

SCHOOL SUBJECTS
Health, Physical education

MINIMUM EDUCATION LEVEL
High school diploma

SALARY RANGE
$15,110 to $38,520 to $100,410+

OUTLOOK
About as fast as the average

OTHER ARTICLES TO READ
Athletic Directors
Physical Education Teachers
Professional Athletes—Individual Sports
Sports Agents
Sports Coaches
Sports Scouts

is common for professional teams to also study other teams' moves and strategies to determine a method of coping with the other teams' plays during a game.

Education and Training

People who hope to become professional athletes should take a full load of high school courses, including four years of English, math, and science as well as health and physical education. College is often the next step in becoming a professional athlete and a strong high school education may help you in earning a college athletic scholarship.

College is important for future professional athletes for several reasons. It provides the opportunity to gain skill and strength in your sport before you try to succeed in the pros, and it offers you the chance of being observed by professional scouts. A college education also provides you with a valuable degree that you can use if you do not earn a living as a professional athlete or after your performance career ends.

Outlook

The employment outlook for professional athletes will vary depending on the sport, its popularity, and the number of positions open with professional teams. On the whole, the outlook for the field of professional sports is healthy and overall employment opportunities are expected to grow about as fast as the average through 2016.

For More Information

To determine if you really want to commit to a career in your team sport, talk to coaches, trainers, and athletes who are currently working in the profession. You can

LeBron James, current star of the Cleveland Cavaliers, is a standout young basketball player. (Associated Press)

also contact professional organizations and associations for information on how to best prepare for a career in their sport.

Amateur Athletic Union
1910 Hotel Plaza Boulevard
Lake Buena Vista, FL 32830-2409
407-934-7200
http://www.aausports.org

American Alliance for Health, Physical Education, Recreation, and Dance
1900 Association Drive
Reston, VA 20191-1598
800-213-7193
info@aahperd.org
http://www.aahperd.org

Property and Casualty Insurance Agents and Brokers

What Property and Casualty Insurance Agents and Brokers Do

Insurance policies were first written so that others could share in the risk of sailing a ship, for example, or of building a factory. Today, *property and casualty insurance agents and brokers* sell insurance policies that help companies and individuals recover the money they have lost due to accidents, thefts, and many other emergencies.

There are three categories of property and casualty insurance salespersons. *Independent agents* work for themselves but represent an insurance company. *Brokers* represent the insurance buyer and order policies either from agents or directly from an insurance company. Both agents and brokers are self-employed, but special agents, called *direct writers*, work for an insurance company and are on that company's payroll.

All three types of salespersons work in a similar way. Their main job is to sell policies, renew and change existing policies, collect premiums, look over their customer's coverage, and help clients report losses and settle claims. Backed by the resources of the companies that they represent, agents may issue policies insuring against loss or damage for everything from furs and automobiles to ocean liners and factories.

Agents attend corporate meetings, keep appointments with individual customers, and spend time in their offices doing research, drafting policies, and handling phone and written correspondence. Agents often are required to work their schedules around their clients' availability, which may mean working three or four nights a week and one or two days on the weekend. Most agents work 40 hours a week, but some agents, particularly those just beginning in the field and those with

SCHOOL SUBJECTS
Business, Mathematics
MINIMUM EDUCATION LEVEL
Some postsecondary training
SALARY RANGE
$25,230 to $44,110 to $113,190
OUTLOOK
More slowly than the average

OTHER ARTICLES TO READ
Insurance Claims Representatives
Insurance Underwriters
Life Insurance Agents and Brokers
Risk Managers

a large clientele, may work 60 hours a week or more.

Education and Training

Property and casualty insurance brokers and agents must have a high school diploma. Many also have college degrees, and some college education is now necessary to succeed in the field. Many colleges and universities offer courses in insurance, and a number of schools offer a bachelor's degree in insurance. Courses in mathematics, economics, business, accounting, and business law are important.

All agents and brokers must have a license in each state in which they sell insurance. Many agents and brokers try to become a Chartered Property Casualty Underwriter (CPCU), which is the highest level they can reach. To receive the CPCU, salespersons must have at least three years of experience and pass a series of examinations.

Outlook

The employment rate of all insurance agents and brokers is expected to grow slower than the average for all occupations through 2016. The overall demand for insurance should be strong as the general population grows and the number of personal and corporate possessions increases. Homeowners and business executives now budget insurance as a necessary expense.

For More Information

Look for opportunities to participate in financial activities. Volunteer to be the treasurer for school clubs or community organizations you belong to. Read books about general business practices, the history of insurance, and the different kinds of insurance available today.

A property and casualty insurance agent explains a policy to his clients. (Rubberball Productions)

American Institute for Chartered Property and Casualty Underwriters
720 Providence Road, Suite 100
Malvern, PA 19355-3433
800-644-2101
customerservice@cpcuiia.org
http://www.aicpcu.org

Independent Insurance Agents & Brokers of America
127 South Peyton Street
Alexandria, VA 22314-2879
800-221-7917
info@iiaba.org
http://www.independentagent.com

Insurance Institute of America
720 Providence Road, Suite 100
Malvern, PA 19355-3433
800-644-2101
customerservice@cpcuiia.org

Property and Real Estate Managers

What Property and Real Estate Managers Do

For most people, real estate is a house or apartment building they own, an apartment or vacation home they rent, or a business they own. For some people and businesses, however, real estate is an investment, similar to stocks. *Property and real estate managers* supervise and control large real estate holdings, manage condominium associations, and purchase and sell real estate for their clients, who own investment property but lack the time or training to manage it.

On-site managers are based at the properties they manage and may even live on the property. Most of them are responsible for apartment buildings. They train, supervise, and assign duties to maintenance staffs; inspect the properties; schedule routine service of heating and air-condi-tioning systems; keep records of operating costs; and submit cost reports to the property managers or owners. They rent vacant space to new tenants and negotiate leases and other rental agreements. They collect rent and make mortgage payments.

Housing project managers direct the operation of housing projects provided for such groups as military families, low-income families, and welfare recipients. The housing is usually subsidized by the government and may consist of single-family homes, multi-unit dwellings, or house trailers.

Some property and real estate managers are hired by condominium associations to manage the condominium property. These managers may be responsible for maintaining swimming pools, community centers, golf courses, parking lots, and common areas in the condominium association's property.

When a business needs new property, either to expand its operations or for investment purposes, it hires a property and real estate manager to find, purchase, and

SCHOOL SUBJECTS
Business, English, Mathematics
MINIMUM EDUCATION LEVEL
Bachelor's degree
SALARY RANGE
$20,800 to $43,670 to $97,890
OUTLOOK
About as fast as the average

OTHER ARTICLES TO READ
Assessors and Appraisers
Real Estate Agents and Brokers
Real Estate Developers
Title Searchers and Examiners

develop that property. The property manager must have good knowledge of property values and current trends in real estate.

Education and Training

Most employers prefer to hire property and real estate managers who have earned a college degree. If you are interested in becoming a property and real estate manager, take college-preparatory courses, including English, business, mathematics, social science, and computer science. In college, you should earn a degree in business administration, finance, real estate, or public administration. Those who enjoy working with people and are patient will have an advantage in this work, since managers frequently are asked to solve problems for residents and tenants.

Various certifications in property management are available from the Institute of Real Estate Management.

Outlook

Employment growth for property and real estate managers is expected to be about as fast as the average through 2016. The best opportunities will be for college graduates with degrees in real estate, business administration, and related fields.

In the next decade, many of the economy's new jobs are expected to be in wholesale and retail trade, finance, insurance, real estate, and other service industries. Growth in these industries will bring a need for more office and retail properties and for people to manage them.

New home developments are increasingly organized with community or homeowner associations that require managers. In addition, more owners of commercial and multi-unit residential properties are expected to use professional managers to help make their properties more profitable.

For More Information

Participate in activities that help you develop management skills, such as serving as an officer in an organization or working on Junior Achievement projects. Volunteer to handle customer service duties for school and community events to get experience with public contact.

Building Owners and Managers Association International
1101 15th Street, NW, Suite 800
Washington, DC 20005-5021
202-408-2662
info@boma.org
http://www.boma.org

Institute of Real Estate Management
430 North Michigan Avenue
Chicago, IL 60611-4011
800-837-0706
custserv@irem.org
http://www.irem.org

 **Did You Know?**

The first property managers, in the early 1900s, were real estate agents who earned additional income by collecting rent and negotiating leases.

Protestant Ministers

What Protestant Ministers Do

Protestant ministers provide for the spiritual, educational, and social needs of Protestant congregations. In most denominations, both men and women serve as ministers. Their primary responsibility is to lead their congregations in worship services, which usually include Bible readings, hymn singing, prayers, and a sermon written and delivered by the minister.

Protestant clergy also administer specific church rites, such as baptism, Holy Communion, christening, and confirmation. They conduct weddings and advise couples concerning the vows and responsibilities of marriage. They may also act as marriage counselors for couples who are having marital difficulties. Ministers conduct funerals, comfort the bereaved, and visit the sick and other congregation members who are unable to come to church.

Protestant ministers play an important part in the religious education of their congregations. They supervise Sunday school and teach confirmation and adult education courses. The extent of their involvement in religious education programs and other church activities often is determined by the size of their congregations. In small churches, ministers may know most of the members personally and take an active role in their day-to-day lives. In larger churches, ministers may have to devote more time to administrative duties and delegate some of their other responsibilities to Sunday school superintendents, deacons, elders, youth pastors, music directors, librarians, secretaries, and others.

Ministers must be outgoing and friendly and have a strong desire to help others. They need patience, sympathy, and open-mindedness to be able to listen to the problems of others while maintaining a discreet and sincere respect.

Education and Training

Protestant ministers usually have a strong feeling that God is calling them to the

SCHOOL SUBJECTS
Religion, Speech

MINIMUM EDUCATION LEVEL
Some postsecondary training

SALARY RANGE
$20,240 to $40,460 to $70,670

OUTLOOK
More slowly than the average

OTHER ARTICLES TO READ
Grief Therapists
Guidance Counselors
Human Services Workers
Psychologists
Social Workers

service of others through religious ministry. If you are interested in becoming a Protestant minister, study history and religion in school. English and speech classes will help improve your communication and speaking skills.

Most Protestant groups require their ministers to have a bachelor's degree plus several years of specialized theological training. Professional study in theological schools generally lasts three years and leads to the Master of Divinity degree.

Outlook

Demand for ministers varies depending on the affiliation, with nondenominational churches needing the most ministers. Aging membership has caused church budgets and membership to shrink, lessening the demand for full-time ministers. Overall, the increased cost of church operations is expected to limit the demand for ministers.

A Protestant minister leads a sermon during church services. (U.S. Census Bureau)

For More Information

Your own minister and church leaders can tell you more about their work, help you determine your own calling, and put you in touch with other people and resources. Become involved with your church as much as possible: teach Sunday school, attend weekly services and Bible study, and help at church events.

Evangelical Lutheran Church in America
8765 West Higgins Road
Chicago, IL 60631
800-638-3522
info@elca.org
http://www.elca.org

Lutheran Church—Missouri Synod
1333 South Kirkwood Road
St. Louis, MO 63122-7295
888-843-5267
http://www.lcms.org

Presbyterian Church (USA)
100 Witherspoon Street
Louisville, KY 40202-1396
888-728-7228
http://www.pcusa.org

Southern Baptist Convention
901 Commerce, Suite 400
Nashville, TN 37203-3699
615-244-2355
http://www.sbc.net

United Methodist Church General Board of Higher Education and Ministry
PO Box 340007
Nashville, TN 37203-0007
800-251-8140
http://www.umc.org

Psychiatric Nurses

What Psychiatric Nurses Do

Psychiatric nurses focus on mental health, including the prevention of mental illness and the maintenance of good mental health, as well as the diagnosis and treatment of mental disorders. They care for pediatric, teen, adult, and elderly patients who may have a broad spectrum of mentally and emotionally related medical needs.

Psychiatric nursing occurs at two levels—basic and advanced. Basic psychiatric nurses are registered nurses who work primarily with patients needing mental health or psychiatric care.

Advanced practice psychiatric nurses are also registered nurses but they have earned certification as certified nurse specialists (CNSs) or have taken graduate courses to become *clinical specialists/nurse practitioners* (CNS/NPs), or *psychiatric nurse practitioners* (PNPs). Some of these specialists may work in supervisory or administrative positions and may, depending on their state's laws,

be able to provide psychotherapy services and prescribe medications. Psychiatric nurses in this more advanced group may specialize in areas such as child-adolescent mental health nursing, geropsychiatric nursing, forensics, or substance abuse.

In addition to direct patient care, some psychiatric nurses may use their training in the community as *community health nurses or educators*. They may also work for insurance or managed-care companies, or in health care institutions or government facilities in an administrative, supervisory, or research position. Other nurses may be self-employed on a consulting or contract basis. Nurses need to display patience, understanding, and composure to help patients during emotional times.

Education and Training

Psychiatric nurses must first be registered nurses. To prepare for this career, you should take high school mathematics and science courses, including biology, chemistry, and physics. Health courses will also be

---

SCHOOL SUBJECTS
Biology, Chemistry

MINIMUM EDUCATION LEVEL
Some postsecondary training

SALARY RANGE
$42,020 to $60,010 to $87,310

OUTLOOK
Faster than the average

OTHER ARTICLES TO READ
Advanced Practice Nurses
Clinical Nurse Specialists
Nurses
Psychiatric Technicians
Psychiatrists
Psychologists

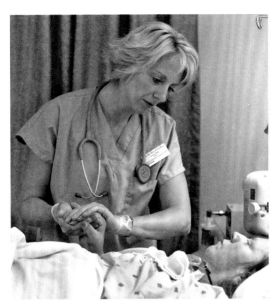

This psychiatric nurse comforts a patient. (Associated Press)

helpful. English and speech courses are important because you must be able to communicate well with patients.

There are three types of training programs available to become a registered nurse: associate's degree, diploma, and bachelor's degree. A bachelor's degree in nursing is required for most supervisory or administrative positions, for jobs in public health agencies, and for admission to graduate nursing programs. A master's degree is usually necessary to prepare for a nursing specialty or to teach. For some specialties, such as nursing research, a Ph.D. is essential.

Usually, some nursing experience is necessary before entering the psychiatric nursing field. Some institutions may require certification as a psychiatric nurse. Psychiatric nurses who are advanced practice nurses and have post-master's degree supervised clinical practice can become certified as specialists in adult or in child and adolescent psychiatric-mental health nursing. Certification is available through the American Nurses Credentialing Center.

All states and the District of Columbia require a license to practice nursing. To obtain a license, graduates of approved nursing schools must pass a national examination. In some states, continuing education is a condition for license renewal.

Outlook

Mental illness is a leading cause of disability in the United States and mental disorders affect one in five Americans. The need for psychiatric nurses will be in great demand in the future. The U.S. Department of Labor projects that employment for registered nurses will grow faster than the average for all occupations through 2016.

For More Information

Volunteer at a local hospital or health care clinic for experience working with patients. Research drug and alcohol dependence, depression, and other mental health topics.

American Association of Colleges of Nursing
One Dupont Circle, NW, Suite 530
Washington, DC 20036-1135
202-463-6930
http://www.aacn.nche.edu

American Nurses Credentialing Center
8515 Georgia Avenue, Suite 400
Silver Spring, MD 20910-3492
800-284-2378
http://www.nursingworld.org/ancc

American Psychiatric Nurses Association
1555 Wilson Boulevard, Suite 530
Arlington, VA 22209
866-243-2443
http://www.apna.org

Psychiatric Technicians

What Psychiatric Technicians Do

Psychiatric technicians work with people who have mental or emotional problems and people who have developmental disabilities. They work at mental hospitals, psychiatric clinics, community mental health centers, and schools for the developmentally disabled. Technicians are also employed by nursing homes, state or general hospitals, child care centers, and social service agencies. Other employers include family service centers, public school counseling services, and schools for the emotionally disturbed.

Technicians work under the supervision of mental health professionals, including psychiatrists, psychologists, and registered nurses. Technicians perform a variety of tasks as they help plan and carry out treatment plans for individual patients. In a hospital setting, they admit, screen, evaluate, or discharge patients. They interview patients and their relatives, keep records, make referrals to community agencies, and work for patients' needs and rights. Technicians watch patients and report their observations to other staff members. They test patients, and they participate in individual or group sessions designed to help patients work out their problems.

After patients are released from a hospital, technicians may visit them at home. They help them adjust to life in their communities. They may help them find a job and a new place to live, if necessary. Above all, technicians try to help each patient function as well as he or she possibly can.

Technicians who work in hospitals may also have nursing duties. They help administer medicines and physical treatments. They can become involved in all parts of their patients' lives—eating and sleeping habits, personal health care, and developing social skills and a better self-image.

Some technicians specialize in one area of mental health care. For example, some work with mentally disturbed children.

SCHOOL SUBJECTS
Biology, Health, Psychology

MINIMUM EDUCATION LEVEL
Some postsecondary training

SALARY RANGE
$19,860 to $29,670 to $47,690

OUTLOOK
More slowly than the average

OTHER ARTICLES TO READ
Home Health Care Aides
Medical Assistants
Medical Laboratory Technicians
Medical Record Technicians
Psychiatrists
Psychologists

Others specialize in working with people who abuse drugs or alcohol. Still others work in community mental health.

Technicians who work with the mentally ill must adjust to an environment that is often chaotic and sometimes upsetting.

Education and Training

Most facilities require psychiatric technicians to have completed a two-year training program after high school. These programs lead to an associate of arts or associate of science degree. These programs include courses on human development, personality structure, and the nature of mental illness. You also study ways to treat people with mental and emotional problems. In addition, you learn how to interview people and how to observe and record patients' behavior. Practical and field learning is an important part of your training. Some states require psychiatric technicians to be licensed. Voluntary certification is available through the American Association of Psychiatric Technicians.

Outlook

Employment for psychiatric technicians is expected to grow slower than the average through 2016. Demand for technicians, though, is expected to continue in large part because of a well-established trend of returning hospitalized patients to their communities after shorter periods of hospitalization. This trend has encouraged development of comprehensive community mental health centers and has led to a strong demand for psychiatric technicians to staff these facilities.

Concerns over rising health care costs should increase employment levels for technicians because they and other paraprofessionals can take over some functions of higher-paid professionals.

For More Information

Volunteer in a health care setting to get experience working with patients and medical professionals. You might also consider volunteering at a local mental health association or a local social welfare agency. Offer to tutor students with disabilities in your school or community.

American Association of Psychiatric Technicians
1220 S Street, Suite 100
Sacramento, CA 95811-7138
800-391-7589
http://www.psychtechs.org

California Association of Psychiatric Technicians
1220 S Street, Suite 100
Sacramento, CA 95811-7138
916-329-9140
http://www.psych-health.com

Psychiatrists

SKILLS SPOTLIGHT

What they do
Communicate ideas
Evaluate and manage information
Help clients and customers

Skills they need
Creative thinking
Decision making
Speaking/listening

What Psychiatrists Do

Psychiatrists are physicians who treat and prevent mental illness. They work with clients who might have feelings of anger or fear, or people who are so confused that they have completely lost touch with reality. Psychiatrists use a variety of methods to treat patients. They might discuss problems, prescribe medicine, or combine discussions, medication, and other types of therapy.

Mental illness has several possible causes. A mental problem might be caused by a physical disorder. It might be caused by a person's inability to handle stress and conflict. Some disorders are only temporary, while others last a long time. People with mental problems cannot do certain things because of the way they think, feel, or act. Whenever possible, psychiatrists help these people overcome their problems and lead happier lives.

To determine the cause of a mental illness, psychiatrists interview patients and give them complete physical examinations.

To understand patients, a psychiatrist must learn about important events in their lives and any strong feelings or opinions they have toward others. Many times a psychiatrist can improve a patient's condition by helping him or her understand why a problem has occurred. Together, the psychiatrist and patient then find other ways for the patient to think and behave. This process is called psychotherapy.

In cases where discussing a problem is not enough, or when serious mental problems are caused by a brain disorder, a psychiatrist may prescribe medication. Drugs that psychiatrists prescribe include mood stabilizers, anti-anxiety drugs, antidepressants, and antipsychotic medications.

Some psychiatrists specialize in treating a particular age group or condition. For example, there are *child psychiatrists* who focus on the problems of youth and their families. *Geriatric psychiatrists* specialize in working with older people. *Industrial psychiatrists* focus on problems that affect em-

SCHOOL SUBJECTS
Biology, Psychology, Sociology

MINIMUM EDUCATION LEVEL
Medical degree

SALARY RANGE
$59,090 to $104,410 to $147,620

OUTLOOK
About as fast as the average

OTHER ARTICLES TO READ
Guidance Counselors
Neurologists
Nurses
Physicians
Psychiatric Technicians
Psychologists
Social Workers

ployee performance, such as alcoholism or absenteeism. *Forensic psychiatrists* evaluate defendants involved in court trials and testify on their mental state.

Education and Training

You need many years of schooling and experience to become a psychiatrist. After you graduate from a four-year college, you must enter a four-year program at a medical school that provides training in anatomy, biology, medical practices, and other subjects. After graduating from medical school, you must pass exams to become a medical doctor.

After you earn your M.D., you must complete at least four additional years of training in the treatment of the mentally ill. You study medical practices, but mostly you train on the job at a psychiatric hospital. You are supervised closely by experienced psychiatrists during this time. Before you can begin to practice as a psychiatrist, you must pass oral and written exams given by the American Board of Psychiatry and Neurology.

Outlook

Employment growth for all physicians should be about as fast as the average through 2016. Opportunities for psychiatrists in private practice and salaried positions are good. Demand is great for child psychiatrists, and other specialties are also in short supply, especially in rural areas and public facilities.

For More Information

Use library and Internet resources to learn all you can about the wide range of mental

Fast Fact

The introduction in the 1950s of medications that could treat conditions such as depression and anxiety greatly increased the patient treatment options for psychiatrists.

and emotional conditions and how they are treated. Volunteer to work in health care settings, such as hospitals, clinics, or nursing homes, to get experience working with patients and medical professionals.

American Psychiatric Association
1000 Wilson Boulevard, Suite 1825
Arlington, VA 22209-3924
888-357-7924
apa@psych.org
http://www.psych.org

National Institute of Mental Health
Public Information and Communications Branch
6001 Executive Boulevard
Room 8184, MSC 9663
Bethesda, MD 20892-9663
301-443-4513
nimhinfo@nih.gov
http://www.nimh.nih.gov

Mental Health America
2000 North Beauregard Street, 6th Floor
Alexandria, VA 22311-1748
703-684-7722
http://www.nmha.org

Psychologists

What Psychologists Do

Psychologists help people by trying to find out why people act and think the way they do. They examine individual and group behavior through testing, experimenting, and studying people's pasts.

Clinical psychologists work with people who have emotional and mental problems. They evaluate and treat a range of difficulties, from family breakups to adolescent rebellion to cases of severe depression and schizophrenia. Clinical psychologists comprise the largest group of specialists. Many clinical psychologists have private practices, where people come to see them in an office. Others are on hospital staffs or college faculties.

Developmental psychologists study the way people grow and change from birth through old age. They describe, measure, and explain age-related changes in behavior, stages of emotional development, universal traits and individual differences, and abnormal changes in development. Many teach and research in colleges and universities, while others specialize in programs for children—in day care centers or preschools, for example—or in programs for the elderly.

Social psychologists study how people deal with each other and with the world around them. They also study many kinds of groups—religious, political, educational, family, and others. Social psychologists may teach in universities or work for private companies or in government.

Counseling psychologists work with people who have problems they find difficult to face alone. These clients are not usually mentally or emotionally ill, but they are emotionally upset, anxious, or struggling with some conflict within themselves or their environment.

School psychologists work with students who have emotional and learning disabilities. They work with those who are having trouble reaching their potential in school,

---

SCHOOL SUBJECTS
Biology, Psychology, Sociology

MINIMUM EDUCATION LEVEL
Master's degree

SALARY RANGE
$36,200 to $79,570 to $128,630

OUTLOOK
Faster than the average

OTHER ARTICLES TO READ
Grief Therapists
Guidance Counselors
Physicians
Psychiatric Nurses
Psychiatric Technicians
Psychiatrists
Rehabilitation Counselors
Social Workers

and they also deal with children whose behavior causes problems in the classroom.

Industrial-organizational psychologists are concerned with the relation between people and work. They deal with organizational structure, worker productivity, job satisfaction, consumer behavior, personnel training and development, and the interaction between humans and machines.

Education and Training

To prepare for a career as a psychologist, concentrate on math, science, and English courses. You should plan on spending from six to 10 years in school after high school. Undergraduate degrees in psychology are designed to prepare you for graduate school. Without a more advanced degree, the kinds of jobs available are limited.

Most psychologists have a doctorate, but some positions are available to those with master's degrees. Clinical psychologists must usually complete one-year internships after receiving their doctorates.

Psychologists who wish to go into private practice in the United States must have a state-issued certificate or license.

Outlook

Employment growth for psychologists is expected to be faster than the average through 2016. The largest increase will be in outpatient mental health and substance abuse treatment clinics. The largest decrease in employment will be in hospital jobs. The outlook is very good for psychologists who are in full-time independent practice. Prospects look best for those who hold doctorates in applied areas, such as clini-

This young girl is attending therapy sessions with a psychologist due to anxiety. (Lewis J. Merrim/Photo Researchers, Inc.)

cal, counseling, health, and industrial/organizational psychology. Competition for jobs will be tougher for those with master's or bachelor's degrees. Most job candidates with bachelor's degrees will not be able to find employment in the psychology field beyond assistant-level jobs.

For More Information

Volunteer at a hospital, clinic, or nursing home to get experience working with patients and check out these associations:

American Psychological Association
750 First Street, NE
Washington, DC 20002-4242
800-374-2721
http://www.apa.org

National Association of School Psychologists
4340 East-West Highway, Suite 402
Bethesda, MD 20814-4460
866-331-6277
http://www.nasponline.org

Public Opinion Researchers

What Public Opinion Researchers Do

Public opinion researchers interview people on the street, in shopping centers, and at other locations, call them on the telephone, or send out questionnaires to find out their preferences, such as what type of soap they buy, what television programs they watch, or how they feel about a particular political issue. The method that researchers use depends on the type of information desired.

Public opinion researchers are involved in selecting the questions to be asked, the people to be asked, asking the questions, and interpreting the results. They conduct these surveys to help business owners, politicians, and others determine how the public feels about certain issues, or what they like or dislike about selected products.

Planning is an important element of developing a questionnaire or other survey technique. Researchers decide what portion of the population they will survey and develop questions that do not force people to answer a certain way.

Researchers who analyze the results often group people together according to age, geographic region, income, ethnicity, education, and other categories. This type of grouping is very popular because it allows those who analyze a survey to suggest how other people with the same characteristics will feel about a topic. It also allows advertisers, politicians, and others to target their products, services, and messages to specific audiences.

Public opinion researchers who conduct interviews must be outgoing and enjoy interacting with a wide variety of people. Because much of the work involves getting people to reveal their personal opinions and beliefs, public opinion researchers are good listeners and nonjudgmental.

Public opinion researchers who work in data analysis must pay close attention to detail and spend long hours analyzing complex data. They may experience some pressure when forced to collect data or solve a problem within a specified period of time. Those who plan questionnaires need good

SCHOOL SUBJECTS
Business, Mathematics, Psychology
MINIMUM EDUCATION LEVEL
Bachelor's degree
SALARY RANGE
$20,400 to $43,910 to $78,940
OUTLOOK
Faster than the average

OTHER ARTICLES TO READ
Demographers
Marketing Researchers
Public Relations Specialists
Sociologists
Telemarketers

analytical skills and a strong command of the English language.

Education and Training

Anyone who interviews people on a regular basis must be friendly and enjoy working with a wide variety of people. Public opinion researchers also need problem solving, data collection, and analysis skills. Courses in English, speech arts, social studies, mathematics (especially statistics), journalism, and psychology are good preparation for this career. Knowledge of a foreign language is also helpful.

A college degree is not always necessary for those who conduct interviews, but researchers involved in developing questions and studying results should have at least a bachelor's degree in economics, business administration, sociology, or psychology. Those who study results need a good background in statistics. Because of the sophisticated techniques used by public opinion researchers, a familiarity with computers is expected, and a master's degree in business administration, sociology, educational psychology, or political science is often required.

Outlook

Employment growth for market and survey research workers is expected to be faster than the average through 2016. Job opportunities should be excellent for people trained in public opinion research, particularly those with graduate degrees. People who specialize in marketing, mathematics, and statistics will have the best opportunities. Marketing research firms, financial services organizations, health care institutions, advertising firms, and insurance firms are potential employers.

Fast Fact

"Push polling" is a telemarketing technique in which the polling firm often does not disclose its true name, and typically asks only one or two often leading questions. The goal of push polling is to "push" voters away from one candidate toward another.

For More Information

If you are involved in student government, you may encounter issues that require a public opinion poll. Your teacher-advisers can help you write fair, unbiased survey questions. Working on your school newspaper also may give you opportunities to interview students, faculty, and parents about a variety of issues.

American Association for Public Opinion Research
PO Box 14263
Lenexa, KS 66285-4263
913-895-4601
info@aapor.org
http://www.aapor.org

American Marketing Association
311 South Wacker Drive, Suite 5800
Chicago, IL 60606-6629
800-262-1150
http://www.marketingpower.com

Marketing Research Association
110 National Drive, 2nd Floor
Glastonbury, CT 06033-1212
860-682-1000
http://www.mra-net.org

Public Relations Specialists

What Public Relations Specialists Do

When a company or an organization wants to present a good image to the public, it turns to its public relations department or to a public relations firm. *Public relations specialists* include executives, writers, artists, and researchers. These specialists work together to provide information to the public about an organization's goals and accomplishments and about its future plans or projects.

Public relations specialists spend much of their time writing. They write reports, news releases, booklets, speeches, copy for radio and television, and film scripts. Public relations specialists also edit employee publications, newsletters, and reports to shareholders. All of this writing and editing has one goal: to offer the public positive information about a person or company.

Contact with the media is another important part of public relations specialists' jobs. They use radio, television, newspapers, and magazines. They also use special events to get their messages across. Press parties, open houses, exhibits at conventions, and speeches help to establish good feelings and a positive image.

Some companies have their own public relations departments and hire their own workers. Other companies hire outside firms whose workers provide public relations services to one or more companies. In either case, public relations specialists work closely with top executives to decide how to keep or improve a company's good image. Public relations workers sometimes do research or conduct public opinion polls. Then they develop a plan and put it into action.

Some public relations workers specialize in one area of public relations. One type of specialized public relations worker is the *lobbyist*. Lobbyists try to persuade elected officials to pass laws that will benefit their clients. For example, the dairy industry

SCHOOL SUBJECTS
English, Journalism
MINIMUM EDUCATION LEVEL
Bachelor's degree
SALARY RANGE
$29,580 to $49,800 to $94,620
OUTLOOK
Faster than the average

OTHER ARTICLES TO READ
Fund-Raisers
Lobbyists
Marketing Researchers
Media Relations Specialists
Press Secretaries
Writers

may hire lobbyists to persuade Congress to write laws favorable to their industry. *Fund-raising directors* develop and direct programs designed to raise funds for social welfare agencies and other nonprofit organizations.

Education and Training

Most public relations specialists are college graduates, so it is important to take college preparatory courses, especially English, speech, humanities, and languages. Writing is an important part of public relations, so you should build your writing skills.

In college, pursue a degree in public relations, English, or journalism. A graduate degree is often required for top managerial positions. Some companies have training programs for newly hired public relations specialists. In other companies, new employees work closely under the supervision of more experienced specialists. They read and file newspaper and magazine articles, research, and learn to write press releases.

Outlook

Employment growth for public relations professionals is expected to be faster than the average through 2016. Competition is strong for beginning jobs in public relations, and people with both education and experience will have an advantage.

For More Information

Almost any experience in working with other people will help you develop strong interpersonal skills, which are crucial in

Paul McCartney (l) has his public relations specialist at his side as he meets with reporters in Tel Aviv, Israel. (Getty Images)

public relations. Join your school newspaper or yearbook staff to work on your writing and reporting skills. Volunteering to help with a political campaign can expose you to how public relations specialists use persuasive speaking and writing tactics and how they deal with the media.

Canadian Public Relations Society, Inc.
4195 Dundas Street West, Suite 346
Toronto, ON M8X 1Y4 Canada
416-239-7034
admin@cprs.ca
http://www.cprs.ca

International Association of Business Communicators
601 Montgomery Street, Suite 900
San Francisco, CA 94111-2612
800-776-4222
service_centre@iabc.com
http://www.iabc.com

Public Relations Society of America
33 Maiden Lane, 11th Floor
New York, NY 10038-5150
212-460-1400
http://www.prsa.org

Public Transportation Operators

What Public Transportation Operators Do

Public transportation operators transport passengers from one location to another by bus, subway, and streetcar. *Bus drivers* operate buses along a route and follow a regular schedule. *Intercity bus drivers* take passengers from one city to another, and *local transit bus drivers* transport passengers within a city. Others drive school buses, airport buses, or tour buses.

Local transit bus drivers usually make stops every block or two along their route. They check passengers' identification cards, give information about schedules and routes, and collect fares.

Intercity bus drivers also pick up and drop off passengers, collect fares, and answer questions. They may have to help collect and load luggage as well. They check safety equipment, such as a fire extinguisher and a first-aid kit, as well as the vehicle's brakes, lights, steering, oil, gas, water, and tires. Bus drivers prepare reports on each trip's mileage, fares, and time, and they also complete reports on accidents or unusual delays. Most bus drivers have to drive on weekends and holidays and at night.

School bus drivers run a predetermined route in the mornings and in the afternoons, transporting students to and from school. Occasionally they drive students and faculty to other events, such as sports competitions or field trips.

Subway drivers and other *local railway system drivers* have many of the same duties as bus drivers. They drive trains that transport passengers throughout cities and suburbs. They usually sit in special compartments at the front of the train where they operate it, starting, slowing, and stopping the train. Rail system drivers obey the signals along their routes, which run underground, at surface levels, or elevated above ground.

Some drivers are assisted by agents, who collect fares and transfers, open and close doors, and announce stops. When

SCHOOL SUBJECTS
Mathematics, Speech
MINIMUM EDUCATION LEVEL
High school diploma
SALARY RANGE
$19,660 to $33,160 to $51,590
OUTLOOK
About as fast as the average

OTHER ARTICLES TO READ
Clerks
Locomotive Engineers
Operating Engineers
Reservation and Ticket Agents
Taxi Drivers
Truck Drivers

Bus drivers make sure riders pay their fares correctly and answer riders' questions so that they can get to where they want to go. (Glenda M. Powers/Shutterstock)

trains malfunction or emergencies occur, drivers contact dispatchers and may have to evacuate passengers from the train cars.

Education and Training

To be a public transportation operator, you need a high school diploma. You must be in good health and have good eyesight, a good driving record, and no criminal record.

Federal regulations require bus drivers to have a commercial, or chauffeur's, license. The U.S. Department of Transportation requires that intercity bus drivers be at least 21 years old and some bus companies hire only drivers that are at least 24 years old. Specific requirements for local bus drivers and rail system operators vary by city.

Outlook

Employment growth for public transportation operators is expected to be as fast as the average for all occupations through 2016. As the population increases, local and intercity travel increases. Future government efforts to reduce traffic and pollution through greater funding of public transportation could also greatly improve job opportunities. Because many of these positions offer relatively high wages and attractive benefits, job seekers may face heavy competition. Those who have good driving records and are willing to work in rapidly growing metropolitan areas will have the best opportunities.

For More Information

Get to know the public transportation system in your city, including bus and train routes. Talk to operators to find out what they like and do not like about their jobs.

Amalgamated Transit Union
5025 Wisconsin Avenue, NW
Washington, DC 20016-4121
202-537-1645
dispatch@atu.org
http://www.atu.org

American Public Transportation Association
1666 K Street, NW, Suite 1100
Washington, DC 20006-1215
202-496-4800
http://www.apta.com

Transport Workers Union of America
1700 Broadway, 2nd Floor
New York, NY 10019-5905
212-259-4900
http://www.twu.com

Purchasing Agents

What Purchasing Agents Do

Purchasing agents buy the raw materials, machinery, supplies, and services for their employers. They usually work for companies that buy more than $100,000 worth of goods each year.

Purchasing agents try to find the best quality materials for the best price. They consider the exact specifications for the required items, cost, quantity discounts, freight handling or other transportation costs, and delivery time. In the past, much of this information was obtained by comparing listings in catalogs and trade journals, interviewing suppliers' representatives, keeping up with current market trends, examining sample goods, and observing demonstrations of equipment. Today, purchasing agents rely on computer databases for their information. Sometimes they visit plants of company suppliers to get a firsthand look at products. After orders are placed, agents follow up to make sure that goods meet the order specifications and that they are delivered on time.

Many purchasing agents specialize in a particular product or field. Procurement engineers buy aircraft equipment. They decide on specifications and requirements for construction, performance, and testing of equipment and are involved in the transactions between buyers and suppliers.

Field contractors purchase fruits, vegetables, and other produce. They may advise growers on methods and supplies to use and help with locating farm labor. Grain buyers manage grain elevators and buy grain for milling. They are concerned with the quality, price, shipping, and storage of grain.

Education and Training

It is possible to become a purchasing agent with only a high school diploma and some related work experience. However, many employers require agents to have a college degree. College work should include courses in general economics, purchasing, accounting, statistics, and business

SCHOOL SUBJECTS
Business, Mathematics
MINIMUM EDUCATION LEVEL
High school diploma
SALARY RANGE
$32,580 to $52,460 to $86,860
OUTLOOK
About as fast as the average

OTHER ARTICLES TO READ
Buyers
Counter and Retail Clerks
Retail Business Owners
Retail Sales Workers
Retail Store Managers
Sales Representatives

❓ Did You Know?

The first purchasing agent jobs emerged during the Industrial Revolution, when manufacturing and business grew and led to the specialization of management jobs.

management. Some colleges and universities offer majors in purchasing, and degrees in business or engineering are also good choices.

Purchasing agents with master's degrees in business administration, engineering, technology, or finance tend to have the best jobs and highest salaries. Companies that manufacture machinery or chemicals may require a degree in engineering or a related field. A civil service examination is required for employment in government purchasing positions.

Outlook

Employment opportunities for purchasing agents are likely to grow about as fast as the average through 2016. Hospitals, schools, state and local governments, and other service-related organizations will be good sources of employment. Demand will be strongest for agents with a master's degree in business administration or an undergraduate degree in purchasing.

Among firms that manufacture complex machinery, chemicals, and other technical products, the demand will be for graduates with a master's degree in engineering, another field of science, or business administration. Graduates of two-year programs in purchasing or materials management should continue to find good opportunities, especially in smaller companies.

For More Information

Join a math club or investment club to learn more about money management and finance. Volunteer to work on committees that are in charge of purchasing supplies and services for special events at your school or church/synagogue. Read periodicals such as *Purchasing* magazine (http://www.purchasing.com) to learn more about the field.

American Purchasing Society
PO Box 256
Aurora Place, IL 60506-0256
630-859-0250
http://www.american-purchasing.com

Institute for Supply Management
PO Box 22160
Tempe, AZ 85285-2160
800-888-6276
http://www.ism.ws

National Institute of Government Purchasing Inc.
151 Spring Street
Herndon, VA 20170-5223
800-367-6447
http://www.nigp.org

Quality Assurance Testers

What Quality Assurance Testers Do

Before computer manufacturers introduce a game, program, or other product to consumers, they first run extensive tests to make sure it works properly. *Quality assurance testers* are the workers who test computer products to ensure they operate at the desired performance level. They also check computer-automated quality assurance programs to confirm that they function properly.

Some testers spend much of their time working on software programs or playing computer games. If it is a game, for example, they play it over and over for hours, trying to make moves quickly or slowly to see if they can crash the program. A program crashes if it completely stops functioning due to, among other things, an inability to process commands. As testers work, they keep close track of the com-

binations they enter so that they can repeat them if the program does crash. They also offer opinions on how user-friendly the program is. Their goal is to make each product more efficient, fun, and visually exciting. Any problems they find are reported to supervisors.

Quality assurance testers give instructions to the computer on which test to administer and to watch the screen for signs of trouble, such as interruption codes and breakdown signals. They also interpret test results, check their accuracy by running them through special programs, and write reports on what they find.

Some quality assurance testers work directly with consumers who have problems with their software. They listen to customer complaints to determine the precise order of keystrokes that led to the problem. Then they repeat the procedure on their own computers and run tests to determine the cause. If the problem is not a result of user-error, they inform programmers and software engineers of the problem and offer suggested solutions.

SCHOOL SUBJECTS
Computer science, Mathematics
MINIMUM EDUCATION LEVEL
High school diploma
SALARY RANGE
$37,180 to $73,750 to $122,180
OUTLOOK
Faster than the average

OTHER ARTICLES TO READ
Computer Programmers
Quality Control Engineers and Technicians
Software Designers
Software Engineers
Systems Setup Specialists
Technical Support Specialists

Fast Fact

The greatest concentration of quality assurance tester jobs are in regions and cities that have software companies, such as the Silicon Valley in northern California, Boston, Chicago, and Atlanta.

Education and Training

A high school diploma is required if you want to work in quality assurance. Most employers offer in-house training. Some do not require postsecondary training, but advanced education helps testers find the best jobs and gain promotion. Some companies require a bachelor's degree in computer science. As the field becomes more competitive, the requirements for finding a job are increasing. The Quality Assurance Institute offers certification in certain areas of quality assurance, including certified quality analyst and certified software test engineer.

Outlook

The number of positions in the field of quality assurance is expected to increase faster than the average through 2016. Fierce competition among software manufacturers is forcing firms to focus their energies on customer service and hire quality assurance testers to make sure their software applications are perfected before they hit the shelves.

For More Information

Learn about computer systems and programs of all kinds, including hardware and software. Look for bugs in your software at home and practice writing them up. Join a computer group or society. Read books on testing, and familiarize yourself with methods, terms, and software development.

IEEE Computer Society
2001 L Street NW, Suite 200
Washington, DC 20036-4910
202-371-0101
http://www.computer.org

Quality Assurance Institute
2101 Park Center Drive, Suite 200
Orlando, FL 32835-7614
407-363-1111
http://www.qaiusa.com

Software & Information Industry Association
1090 Vermont Avenue, NW, 6th Floor
Washington, DC 20005-4095
202-289-7442
http://www.siia.net

Software Testing Institute
http://www.softwaretestinginstitute.com

Quality Control Engineers and Technicians

SKILLS SPOTLIGHT

What they do
Evaluate and manage information
Help clients and customers
Select and apply tools/technology

Skills they need
Mathematics
Problem solving
Reading/writing

What Quality Control Engineers and Technicians Do

Quality control engineers develop, implement, and direct processes and practices that help ensure the quality of manufactured parts. They set standards to measure the quality of a part or product, analyze factors that affect quality, and determine the best practices to guarantee quality.

Quality control engineers are concerned with effective manufacturing procedures, productivity, and cost factors. They focus on ensuring quality during production operations, and they also get involved in product design and evaluation. They work with manufacturing engineers and industrial designers during the design phase of a product, and they work with sales and marketing professionals to evaluate reports from consumers on how well a product is performing.

Quality control engineers make sure that all materials used in a finished product meet required standards and that all instruments and automated equipment used to test and monitor parts during production perform properly. They supervise and direct workers involved in assuring quality, including quality control technicians, inspectors, and production personnel.

Quality control technicians work with quality control engineers in designing, implementing, and maintaining quality systems. They test and inspect materials and products during all phases of production to make sure they meet specified levels of quality. They test random samples of products or monitor production workers and automated testing equipment that inspect products during manufacturing. Using engineering blueprints, drawings, and specifications, they measure and inspect parts for dimensions, performance, and mechanical, electrical, and chemical properties. They establish tolerances, or acceptable deviations

SCHOOL SUBJECTS
Mathematics, Physics
MINIMUM EDUCATION LEVEL
Bachelor's degree (engineers)
Associate's degree (technicians)
SALARY RANGE
$47,630 to $85,260 to $126,180 (engineers)
$31,630 to $56,060 to $79,900 (technicians)
OUTLOOK
About as fast as the average

OTHER ARTICLES TO READ
Construction Inspectors
Manufacturing Supervisors
Papermaking Workers
Quality Assurance Testers

from engineering specifications, and they direct manufacturing personnel in identifying rejects and items that need to be reworked. They monitor production processes to be sure that machinery and equipment are working properly and set to established specifications.

Education and Training

Quality control engineers must have a bachelor's degree in engineering. Many quality control engineers receive degrees in industrial or manufacturing engineering. Some receive degrees in metallurgical, mechanical, electrical, or chemical engineering, depending on where they plan to work.

Education and training requirements vary for quality control technicians in different industries. In the food processing industry, technicians may need only good mathematics and reading skills. But in many other industries, such as the drug industry, more training is required. Many community colleges and technical institutes offer two-year training programs that teach sciences, mathematics, engineering, statistics, design and production, and

Quality control technician Frank Pantaleon checks samples at his lab. (Getty Images)

other subjects related to testing the quality of materials.

Outlook

Although many economists forecast low to moderate growth in manufacturing operations through 2016, employment opportunities for quality control personnel should grow about as fast as the average as many companies place increased emphasis on quality control activities.

Many companies are making vigorous efforts to make their manufacturing processes more efficient, lower costs, and improve productivity and quality. Opportunities for quality control engineers and technicians should be good in the food and beverage industries, pharmaceutical firms, electronics companies, and chemical companies. Employment should also be good in the aerospace, biomedical, bioengineering, environmental controls, and transportation industries.

For More Information

Take industrial arts courses that introduce you to different kinds of scientific or technical equipment. Join a radio, computer, or science club to get experience in team-building and problem-solving activities.

American Society for Quality
600 North Plankinton Avenue
Milwaukee, WI 53203-4839
800-248-1946
help@asq.org
http://www.asq.org

ASTM International
100 Barr Harbor Drive
PO Box C700
West Conshohocken, PA 19428-2959
610-832-9500
http://www.astm.org

Rabbis

What Rabbis Do

Rabbis are the spiritual leaders of Jewish congregations. They interpret Jewish law and tradition and conduct religious services on the Sabbath and holy days. Rabbis officiate at weddings, funerals, and other rites of passage in the Jewish tradition, counsel members of the congregation, visit the sick, and take part in community and interfaith affairs. Rabbis further serve their congregations by supervising and teaching religious education courses.

Within Judaism, the rabbi has an elevated status in spiritual matters, although most Jewish synagogues and temples have a relatively democratic form of decision making in which many members participate. Rabbis of large congregations spend much of their time working with their staffs and various committees. They often receive assistance from an associate or assistant rabbi.

Smaller synagogues may have only one rabbi, while larger synagogues may have a *chief rabbi* and one or more *assistant rabbis*. Most congregations also have a *cantor*, or *hazzan*, who leads liturgies and prayers. Cantors are trained in both music and religious education. Both rabbis and professional cantors are ordained clergy, and both have the authority to conduct weddings, funerals, visit sick synagogue members, and teach adult education classes.

Many rabbis take on additional responsibilities in the community at large. They may become involved with such social concerns as poverty, community relations, or drug abuse, or they may take part in interfaith activities with ministers of other religions.

Some rabbis do not serve as congregational leaders but instead serve as educators at schools and seminaries, as writers and scholars, or as chaplains at hospitals or in the armed forces.

A primary consideration in choosing a career in the clergy is a strong religious faith coupled with the desire to help others. Rabbis should be able to communicate effectively and supervise others. They must have self-confidence, initiative, and the ability to deal with pressure. They need to

---

SCHOOL SUBJECTS
Foreign language, Religion

MINIMUM EDUCATION LEVEL
Master's degree

SALARY RANGE
$20,240 to $40,460 to $70,670

OUTLOOK
Faster than the average

OTHER ARTICLES TO READ
Grief Therapists
Historians
Psychologists
Social Workers

Fast Fact

be impartial when listening to the troubles and worries of congregants. They must be tactful and compassionate in order to deal with people of many backgrounds. They must set a high moral and ethical standard for the members of their congregations.

Education and Training

If you hope to become a rabbi, take all religious and Hebrew language courses available to you. You need to complete a bachelor's degree before entering a seminary. Degrees in Jewish studies, philosophy, English, and history can fulfill seminary entrance requirements. Completion of a course of study in a seminary is a prerequisite for ordination as a rabbi.

Most seminary programs lead to the Master of Arts in Hebrew Letters degree and ordination as a rabbi. Most programs last about five years, and many of them include a period of study in Jerusalem.

Outlook

Job opportunities for rabbis are good in all the major branches of Judaism. Orthodox rabbis should have good job prospects as older rabbis retire and smaller communities become large enough to hire their own rabbis. Conservative and Reform rabbis should also have excellent employment opportu-

nities, especially because of retirement and new Jewish communities. Reconstructionist rabbis should find very good opportunities because this branch of Judaism is growing rapidly.

For More Information

Talk with your own rabbi and others involved in the work of the synagogue or temple to get a clearer idea of the rewards and responsibilities of this profession. You should be able to find volunteer opportunities at your synagogue as well. Most Jewish seminaries are also eager to work with young people to help them learn about the rabbinate before making a firm decision about it.

Central Conference of American Rabbis (Reform)
355 Lexington Avenue
New York, NY 10017-0003
212-972-3636
info@ccarnet.org
http://ccarnet.org

Jewish Reconstructionist Federation
Beit Devora
101 Greenwood Ave. Suite 430
Jenkintown, PA 19046-2637
215-885-5601
http://www.jrf.org

Rabbinical Assembly (Conservative)
3080 Broadway
New York, NY 10027-4650
212-280-6000
info@rabbinicalassembly.org
http://www.rabbinicalassembly.org

Rabbinical Council of America (Orthodox)
305 Seventh Avenue, 12th Floor
New York, NY 10001-6008
212-807-9000
office@rabbis.org
http://rabbis.org

Radio and Television Announcers

SKILLS SPOTLIGHT

What they do
Communicate ideas
Evaluate and manage information
Work with a team

Skills they need
Creative thinking
Reading/writing
Speaking/listening

What Radio and Television Announcers Do

Radio and television announcers are the people who read the names and call letters of stations, announce station breaks, introduce and close shows, and make public service announcements. Radio announcers interview guests or moderate panel discussions. In some smaller stations, the announcer is also responsible for keeping the station log, running the transmitter, and writing news and other scripts.

Announcers have many specialized roles. For example, *disc jockeys* play music interspersed with commercial messages and talk. They sometimes read the news, weather forecasts, and traffic reports. Except for advertisements and news reports, most of their talk is unscripted and conversational.

Sportscasters cover sports events for the radio and television audience. These an-

nouncers have specialized knowledge of the sporting events they cover and are able to announce quickly and accurately what is happening during the event. Fast-moving sports such as hockey and basketball require a sportscaster who can describe the important events rapidly and without confusion.

Newscasters specialize in reporting the news, including regional, national, and international events. Some newscasters also provide editorial commentary and personal opinions on news events and issues. In some instances, newscasters write their own scripts based on facts that are furnished by international news bureaus. In other instances, they read text exactly as it comes in. They may make as few as one or two reports each day if they work on a major news program, or they may broadcast news for five minutes every hour or half-hour. Newscasters may specialize in certain aspects of the news, such as economics, politics, health and medicine, or military activity.

SCHOOL SUBJECTS
English, Speech

MINIMUM EDUCATION LEVEL
Some postsecondary training

SALARY RANGE
$14,790 to $26,060 to $75,020

OUTLOOK
Decline

OTHER ARTICLES TO READ
Broadcast Engineers
Disc Jockeys
Radio and Television Program Directors
Radio Producers
Sportswriters
Writers

These three radio announcers host a morning show on local radio. (FEMA)

News anchors are the primary announcers for half-hour or hour-long news programs and special news coverage. They read the main news events and then introduce reporters who give more detailed coverage, including interviews and film clips.

Education and Training

Most large radio and television stations prefer to hire announcers who have a bachelor's degree. Some trade schools offer programs in radio and television announcing, but you should investigate programs thoroughly before you enroll. Some of these programs are expensive and may offer little valuable training. You might talk to local radio or television station managers to get their opinions on which programs will be helpful and which ones to avoid.

Outlook

Competition for entry-level employment in announcing during the coming years is expected to be strong, as the broadcasting industry always attracts more applicants than are needed. There is a better chance of working in radio than in television because there are more radio stations. Local television stations usually carry a high percentage of network programs and need only a very small staff to carry out local operations. The top television markets are New York, Los Angeles, Chicago, Philadelphia, and San Francisco.

There is little new growth in the number of new radio and television stations so most job openings will result from people leaving the industry or the labor force. Newscasters who specialize in such areas as business, consumer, and health news should have an advantage over other job applicants.

For More Information

Practice your public speaking skills. Join a speech, debate, or forensics club. Take tours of local radio and television stations.

Association of Public Television Stations
2100 Crystal Drive, Suite 700
Arlington, VA 22202-3784
202-654-4200
http://www.apts.org

National Association of Broadcast Employees and Technicians
501 Third Street, NW
Washington, DC 20001-2797
202-434-1100
cwaweb@cwa-union.org
http://nabetcwa.org

National Association of Broadcasters
1771 N Street, NW
Washington, DC 20036-2800
202-429-5300
nab@nab.org
http://www.nab.org

Radio and Television Program Directors

What Radio and Television Program Directors Do

Radio and television program directors plan and schedule programs for radio and television stations and networks. They work in both commercial and public broadcasting and work for individual radio or television stations, regional or national networks, or cable television systems.

Program directors work on entertainment programs, public service programs, newscasts, sportscasts, and commercial announcements. Program directors decide what material is broadcast and when it is scheduled. They work with other staff members to develop programs and buy programs from independent producers. They are guided by such factors as the budget available for program material, the audience their station or network wants to attract, their organization's policies on content and other matters, and the kinds of products advertised in the various commercial announcements. It is important for program directors to understand their listeners, viewers, advertisers, and sponsors and be able to adapt programming to their needs and goals.

Program directors also set schedules for the program staff, audition and hire announcers and other on-the-air personnel, and assist the sales department in negotiating contracts with sponsors of commercial announcements. The duties of individual program directors depend on whether they work in radio or television, the size of the organization, whether they work for one station or a network, or whether it is a commercial or public operation.

Some larger stations and networks employ *public service directors* to plan and schedule radio or television public service programs and announcements in such fields as education, religion, and civic and government affairs. *Broadcast operations*

SCHOOL SUBJECTS
Business, Journalism
MINIMUM EDUCATION LEVEL
Bachelor's degree
SALARY RANGE
$28,980 to $61,090 to $96,670
OUTLOOK
About as fast as the average
OTHER ARTICLES TO READ
Broadcast Engineers
Disc Jockeys
Radio and Television Announcers
Radio Producers
Reporters

directors coordinate the activities of the personnel who prepare network program schedules, review program schedules, issue daily corrections, and advise affiliated stations on their schedules. Other managers in radio and television broadcasting include *production managers*, *operations directors*, *news directors*, and *sports directors*.

Education and Training

English, debate, and speech classes are good preparation for this career. Business courses are also helpful.

A college degree is recommended for this field. Possible majors for those interested in this work include radio and television production and broadcasting, communications, liberal arts, or business administration. Technical training will help you understand the engineering aspects of broadcasting. Experience at a radio or television station is important. Many program directors move into their positions after working for a number of years as a music director, as a staff announcer, or in some other capacity at a station.

Outlook

Generally, employment growth in radio and television broadcasting is expected to be about as fast as the average for all industries through 2016. The growth rate is attributed to expanding cable and satellite television operations, and the continued growth of interactive media.

For More Information

Get any experience you can with radio or television broadcasting, such as volunteering to help at small radio stations or local cable stations. Take tours of large stations

 Fast Fact

In addition to ranking the number of viewers a television show gets, Nielsen ranks the size of television markets. The top five markets in the United States are New York, Los Angeles, Chicago, Philadelphia, and San Francisco/Oakland/San Jose.

in your area. Volunteer to work on school committees in charge of planning and directing special events.

Association of Public Television Stations
2100 Crystal Drive, Suite 700
Arlington, VA 22202-3784
202-654-4200
http://www.apts.org

National Association of Broadcasters
1771 N Street, NW
Washington, DC 20036-2800
202-429-5300
nab@nab.org
http://www.nab.org

National Cable & Telecommunications Association
25 Massachusetts Avenue, NW, Suite 100
Washington, DC 20001-1413
202-222-2300
http://www.ncta.com

Radio-Television News Directors Association
1025 F Street, NW, 7th Floor
Washington, DC 20004 -1412
202-659-6510
http://www.rtnda.org

Radio Producers

SKILLS SPOTLIGHT
What they do
Communicate ideas
Evaluate and manage information
Exercise leadership

Skills they need
Decision making
Problem solving
Speaking/listening

What Radio Producers Do

Radio producers plan, rehearse, and produce live or recorded programs. They work with on-air personnel, behind-the-scenes workers, music, sound effects, and technology to put together a radio show. In many situations, particularly with smaller radio stations, the disc jockey and the show's producer are the same person.

Radio producers study the marketplace by listening to other area radio stations and determining what's needed and appreciated in the community. They conduct surveys and interviews to find out what the public wants to hear. They decide which age groups they want to pursue and develop a format based on what appeals to these listeners.

Based on listener feedback and on market research, radio disc jockeys and producers determine what music to play and create music libraries that will help the station develop a unique on-air identity.

Producers also keep track of current events. They consult newspapers and radio programs to determine what subjects to discuss on their shows.

Producers have to keep a show running on time, which involves carefully weaving many elements into a show, including music, news reports, interviews, and commercials. They write copy for and coordinate on-air commercials, which are usually recorded in advance. They also devise contests, from large public events to small, on-air trivia competitions.

Though a majority of radio stations have music formats, radio producers also work for 24-hour news stations, public broadcasting, and talk radio. Producing news programs and radio documentaries involves a great deal of research, booking guests, writing scripts, and interviewing.

Education and Training

Writing skills are especially valuable if you want to work in radio. Take English and social science courses that require essays and term papers. Journalism classes will not only help you develop your writing skills

SCHOOL SUBJECTS
English, Journalism, Speech
MINIMUM EDUCATION LEVEL
Bachelor's degree
SALARY RANGE
$28,980 to $61,090 to $96,670
OUTLOOK
About as fast as the average

OTHER ARTICLES TO READ
Disc Jockeys
Radio and Television Announcers
Radio and Television Program Directors
Radio Producers

but also teach you about the nature and history of media.

After high school, look for universities with schools of journalism or communications that offer programs in broadcasting. Business courses will help you prepare for a career as a producer. Radio producers often start their training in journalism schools and receive hands-on instruction at campus radio stations. News directors and program managers of radio stations generally want to hire people who have a well-rounded education with knowledge of history, geography, political science, and literature.

Outlook

Employment growth in the radio industry is expected to be about as fast as the average through 2016. Today, radio stations are bought and sold at a rapid pace. Mergers often result in radio stations having to change formats as well as entire staffs. Though some radio producers are able to stay at a station over a period of several years, people going into radio should be prepared to change employers at some point in their careers.

Another trend that is affecting radio producing jobs is the increasing use of programming created by services outside the broadcasting industry. Satellite radio, in which subscribers pay a monthly fee for access to 100 or more radio stations, will be a big threat to smaller, marginal stations.

Competition is stiff for all radio jobs. Graduates of college broadcasting programs are finding a scarcity of work in media. Paid internships will also be difficult to find; many students of radio will have to work for free for a while to gain experience.

For More Information

Small radio stations may be willing to let young, inexperienced people work behind the scenes. Some high schools have on-site radio stations that allow students to get hands-on experience. You can develop valuable skills by getting involved in management and planning for any clubs you belong to.

Broadcast Education Association
1771 N Street, NW
Washington, DC 20036-2891
202-429-3935
http://www.beaweb.org

National Association of Broadcasters
1771 N Street, NW
Washington, DC 20036-2800
202-429-5300
nab@nab.org
http://www.nab.org

Railroad Conductors

What Railroad Conductors Do

A *railroad conductor* is the person who yells "All aboard!" in movies and on television, but real-life conductors have much more responsibility than that. Conductors are in charge of the entire train, including other train employees and all the train equipment. On trains today, a conductor and the locomotive engineer may be the only crew members aboard the train.

Some railroad conductors, called *road conductors*, supervise trains that carry passengers and freight. *Yard conductors* work in rail yards, directing workers on switching crews that put together and take apart trains.

Conductors who work on freight trains keep track of each car's cargo. They make sure cars are dropped off or picked up at certain stops. They also inspect the cars to be certain that they are in good condition and properly sealed.

Conductors who work on passenger trains attend to the comfort and safety of passengers. They oversee the boarding of passengers and collect tickets and fares. At stops, they help passengers get off the train safely and tell the engineer when to pull away from the station. If there is an accident, conductors take charge of the situation.

On both passenger and freight trains, conductors are in constant contact with the locomotive engineer. Before departing, they go over schedules and times with the engineer. During the run, conductors may receive information over the radio about track conditions or special instructions. They may also monitor information about any problems with the train's operation and pass that information along to the engineer using a two-way radio.

When working in rail yards, conductors make sure that trains are put together and ready to go on time. They throw switches to direct cars to certain tracks for unloading.

SCHOOL SUBJECTS
Computer science, Technical/Shop

MINIMUM EDUCATION LEVEL
Apprenticeship

SALARY RANGE
$37,490 to $58,650 to $92,550

OUTLOOK
Decline

OTHER ARTICLES TO READ
Clerks
Flight Attendants
Locomotive Engineers
Merchant Mariners
Public Transportation Operators
Reservation and Ticket Agents

Railroad conductors help to keep their trains running on schedule. (Frances L. Fruit/Shutterstock)

They tell switching crews which cars to put together and which ones to take apart.

Education and Training

A high school education is required to enter this field. Machine shop and electrical shop classes are good choices for future conductors. Computer science is also helpful.

A railroad conductor position is not an entry-level job. Most conductors gain experience by working different jobs for the railroad and after years of experience they are promoted to conductors.

To be a conductor, you must pass an entrance-to-service medical examination and periodic physicals throughout your career. You are also required to take tests that screen for drug use. You must be able to lift 80 pounds, as required when replacing knuckles—heavy metal couplings that connect rail cars.

Outlook

Job opportunities for railroad conductors are expected to decline. Rail passenger services to many points have been discontinued. Although the volume of railroad freight business is expected to increase in the coming years, the use of automation and larger, faster trains is expected to cause a continued decline in the employment of rail transportation workers. Computers are now used to keep track of empty freight cars, match empty cars with the closest load, and dispatch trains. Also, new work rules that allow two- and three-person crews instead of the traditional five-person crews are becoming more widely used, and these factors combine to lessen the need for conductors and other crew workers.

For More Information

A visit to a rail yard might give you some insight into the work of a yard conductor and into the operations of railroads in general. Visit one of the many railroad museums around the country, and search the Internet for sites related to railroads. There is a large community of railroad enthusiasts, so you might be able to find a club in your area.

American Short Line and Regional Railroad Association
50 F Street, NW, Suite 7020
Washington, DC 20001-1507
202-628-4500
aslrra@aslrra.org
http://www.aslrra.org

Association of American Railroads
50 F Street, NW
Washington, DC 20001-1564
202-639-2100
http://www.aar.org

Federal Railroad Administration
1200 New Jersey Avenue, SE
Washington, DC 20590-0001
http://www.fra.dot.gov

Range Managers

SKILLS SPOTLIGHT

What they do
Allocate funds and resources
Evaluate and manage information
Exercise leadership

Skills they need
Decision making
Problem solving
Responsibility

What Range Managers Do

Range managers help protect the environment and improve and increase the food supply on ranges, which cover more than 1 billion acres of land in the western United States and Alaska. Range managers also may be called *range scientists*, *range ecologists*, and *range conservationists*.

Ranges are the source of food for both livestock and wildlife, but overgrazing by animals can leave the land bare. When there is neither grass nor shrubs on open land, soil erosion occurs. Range managers are in charge of erosion-control programs, such as irrigation and rotating grazing lands.

Range managers study rangelands to decide the number and kinds of cattle that can best graze on these lands and the times of year that are best for grazing. They also study different varieties of plants to determine which ones will grow best and which

might actually be harmful to the land and its wildlife.

Range managers try to conserve the land for a variety of other uses, such as outdoor recreation, timber, and habitats for many kinds of wildlife. They look for ways to prevent damage by fire and rodents. If a fire does occur, range managers try to restore the land. They make sure fences and corrals are in good condition and water reservoirs are well maintained.

Most range managers work in the western part of the United States or in Alaska, where most of the nation's rangelands are located. Most range managers work for the federal government in the Forest Service, the Natural Resource Conservation Service of the Department of Agriculture, the Bureau of Indian Affairs, or the Bureau of Land Management of the Department of the Interior. Other employers include state governments and oil and coal companies, which need experts to help repair the land damaged by mining and exploring for oil.

SCHOOL SUBJECTS
Biology, Earth science

MINIMUM EDUCATION LEVEL
Bachelor's degree

SALARY RANGE
$34,620 to $58,000 to $100,800

OUTLOOK
More slowly than the average

OTHER ARTICLES TO READ
Agribusiness Technicians
Agricultural Scientists
Ecologists
Land Trust or Preserve Managers
Naturalists
Park Rangers
Soil Scientists

Fast Fact

Rangelands cover more than one billion acres in the United States.

Education and Training

To prepare for a career as a range manager, take classes in biology, chemistry, physics, and mathematics. Business classes also will be helpful for learning aspects of management. Range managers must have a bachelor's degree in range science, soil science, or natural resource management. For many range manager positions you need a graduate degree in one of these fields. About 35 colleges and universities have degree programs in range management or range science or in another discipline with a range management or range science option.

The Society for Range Management offers voluntary certification as a Certified Range Management Consultant or a Certified Professional in Rangeland Management. Contact the society for more information.

Outlook

Job growth will be slower than the average through 2016 for conservation scientists and foresters, a category that includes range managers. Large ranches will continue to employ range managers to improve range management practices and increase output and profitability. Range specialists may find more opportunities in private industry to advise on the reclamation of lands damaged by oil and coal exploration. A small number of new jobs will result from the need for range and soil conservationists to provide technical assistance to owners of grazing land through the Natural Resource Conservation Service. An additional demand for range managers could be created by the conversion of rangelands to other purposes, such as wildlife habitats and recreation.

For More Information

Volunteer to work with conservation organizations or with parks and land preserves in your area. Look for a summer job on a farm or range.

Society for Range Management
10030 West 27th Avenue
Wheat Ridge, CO 80215-6601
303-986-3309
srmweb@rangelands.org
http://www.rangelands.org

U.S. Department of Agriculture
Forest Service
1400 Independence Avenue, SW
Washington, DC 20250-1111
800-832-1355
http://www.fs.fed.us/

U.S. Department of the Interior
Bureau of Land Management
1849 C Street, Room 5665
Washington, DC 20240-0001
202-208-3801
woinfo@blm.gov
http://www.blm.gov

Real Estate Agents and Brokers

What Real Estate Agents and Brokers Do

Purchasing a home is an important decision, so people often seek the help of real estate agents and brokers when they buy or sell a house. *Real estate agents and brokers* assist people in the process of buying and selling property, and they act as intermediaries in the price negotiations between buyer and seller. Because they understand the legal steps necessary to complete a sale and know how to get mortgage loans, agents and brokers provide the expertise that many people need when they buy or sell a piece of property.

When a person decides to sell a house, he or she usually contacts a licensed real estate agent. The agent visits the property to get a good idea of what the property is worth and to identify some of the most desirable features that will attract prospective buyers. Frequently, the agent or broker counsels the owner on what price to ask for the home. The owner then usually signs a contract agreeing to pay the agent a standard percentage of the selling price if the agent sells the property within a specified amount of time.

When a client is interested in buying a home, the agent interviews the client to understand what type of home he or she is looking for. The agent then consults home listings to see what is available and takes the potential buyer to see homes that meet his or her needs and income.

Although most people have common questions concerning price and home construction, each client is looking for different qualities in a home, and agents must adjust their recommendations based on those needs.

In addition to spending a great deal of time showing homes to prospective buyers, agents spend a lot of time on the telephone seeking new home listings and finding the answers to clients' financial questions and

SCHOOL SUBJECTS
Business, English, Mathematics
MINIMUM EDUCATION LEVEL
High school diploma
SALARY RANGE
$20,930 to $40,600 to $106,790 (agents) $25,990 to $37,500 to $100,570 (brokers)
OUTLOOK
More slowly than the average

OTHER ARTICLES TO READ
Assessors and Appraisers
Financial Planners
Property and Real Estate Developers
Title Searchers and Examiners

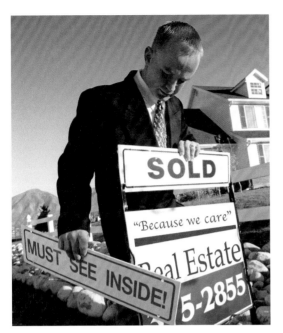

A real estate agent places a sign on the front lawn of a home he just sold. (Rubberball Productions)

other concerns. Agents also use computers to provide up-to-date information on changing neighborhoods, new mortgage rates, and other related topics.

Education and Training

Although there are no specific educational requirements, most agents should have at least some college training. Many colleges and universities offer four-year degrees in real estate, which may be helpful for entering a career in real estate.

All real estate agents and brokers must pass a written examination covering real estate principles and laws affecting the sale of property before being licensed to practice. Most states require agents applying for a license to complete at least 30 hours of classroom instruction; those seeking a

broker's license must usually complete 90 hours of formal training.

Outlook

Employment growth for agents and brokers is expected to be slower than the average through 2016. Turnover within the field is high; new job opportunities open as agents retire or transfer to other types of work. The field of real estate is easily affected by changes in the economy. Periods of prosperity bring a lot of business. Conversely, a downturn leads to a lower number of real estate transactions, resulting in fewer sales and commissions for agents and brokers.

For More Information

Contact local real estate brokers and agents for useful information on the field. You can also obtain information on licensing requirements from local real estate boards or from the real estate departments of each state.

Association of Real Estate License Law Officials
8361 Sangre De Cristo Road, Suite 250
Littleton, CO 80127-4238
303-979-6140
mailbox@arello.org
http://www.arello.org

National Association of Realtors
430 North Michigan Avenue
Chicago, IL 60611-4087
800-874-6500
http://www.realtor.org

Society of Industrial and Office Realtors
1201 New York Avenue, NW, Suite 350
Washington, DC 20005-6126
202-449-8200
admin@sior.com
http://www.sior.com

Real Estate Assessors and Appraisers

What Real Estate Assessors and Appraisers Do

Real estate assessors and appraisers estimate the value of land, residences, commercial buildings, and other real property. Their estimates are used to establish property taxes, confirm mortgage agreements, provide sales prices, and for a variety of reasons.

Appraisers and assessors generate detailed written descriptions of the properties they are valuing. Oftentimes they take photographs of the property to document the physical conditions described in their reports. They may use standardized checklists to assist in the evaluation process.

In general, appraisers work for a single company or as independent, self-employed consultants, determining the value of one property at a time. They may specialize in one type of real estate such as homes, shopping malls, or farmland.

Assessors usually work for a municipal government to establish all the property values in a locality for tax purposes. They are responsible for issuing notices regarding taxes. Assessors must be knowledgeable on local and state tax codes and procedures especially in instances where property owners contest their assessments. Usually the *senior assessor* is an elected position.

Education and Training

High school courses in English and mathematics will prepare you for writing reports and calculating values. Take courses to help develop your keyboarding and computer skills.

Until recently there were no formal education degree requirements for real estate appraisers and assessors. Today, however, both appraisers and assessors must have at minimum a bachelor's degree as part of state licensure and/or certification requirements. Although there is no mandatory

---

SCHOOL SUBJECTS
Computer science, English, Mathematics

MINIMUM EDUCATION LEVEL
Some postsecondary training

SALARY RANGE
$24,000 to $44,460 to $86,140

OUTLOOK
Faster than the average

OTHER ARTICLES TO READ
Assessors and Appraisers
Construction Inspectors
Land Acquisition Professionals
Real Estate Developers

Growth Field

Between 2006 and 2016 the number of real estate assessors and appraisers is expected to grow from 101,000 to 118,000, an increase of about 17 percent.

degree area, a focus on economics, finance, or real estate is highly recommended.

The licensing and certification process also includes on-the-job training, including time as a trainee, and passing an examination. Additional requirements vary by state.

Outlook

Growth opportunities for real estate appraisers and assessors is expected be faster than the average. Those licensed and experienced should be well positioned for the best jobs.

With increased attention on foreclosure activities, appraisers and assessors will be needed to evaluate the rising number of property transactions. Self-employed appraisers will probably see the most demand as financial institutions contract out work for loan appraisals.

For More Information

Contact your local tax assessors office for useful information on the field as well as for state licensing requirements.

American Society of Appraisers
555 Herndon Parkway, Suite 125
Herndon, VA 20170-5276
800-272-8258
http://www.appraisers.org

Appraisal Institute
550 West Van Buren Street, Suite 1000
Chicago, IL 60607-3827
312-335-4400
http://www.appraisalinstitute.org

International Association of Assessing Officers
314 West 10th Street
Kansas City, MO 64105-1616
816-701-8100
http://www.iaao.org

Real Estate Developers

SKILLS SPOTLIGHT

What they do
Communicate ideas
Evaluate and manage information
Exercise leadership

Skills they need
Decision making
Responsibility
Speaking/listening

What Real Estate Developers Do

Real estate developers plan and direct construction or renovation of buildings for commercial or private use. This process involves negotiation with property owners, real estate agents, investors, lending institutions such as banks and insurance companies, architects, lawyers, general contractors, government officials, and other parties. Developers may work independently as consultants or in partnership with professionals involved in real estate development.

A developer may be involved in purchasing suburban acres and developing condominiums, a park, a golf course, or a shopping center. Or a developer may renovate an existing structure such as a warehouse, turning it into a restaurant or office space. The day-to-day duties of a developer vary depending on the development entity. A development entity consists of the owner of the project (the person who will profit or suffer losses from the development), the investors who put up the initial funding, and the developer.

At the beginning of a project the developer negotiates with a variety of people to obtain funding for the project. Without these funds, a developer will not get financing to finish the project. Many times, the government will help with financing if the project benefits the community at large. Such projects include the construction of stadiums and improvement of infrastructure, such as the widening of streets.

Developers must complete a series of steps and work with a variety of people to complete their projects. They must complete an impact study of how their project will affect the community and the environment. They may meet with a zoning board to ensure that all regulations are being met. Developers hire architects to create building plans that they submit to the building department for approval. While they wait for approval, developers put the plans out for bids from general contractors who, if

SCHOOL SUBJECTS
Business, Mathematics

MINIMUM EDUCATION LEVEL
High school diploma

SALARY RANGE
$20,800 to $43,670 to $97,890

OUTLOOK
More slowly than the average

OTHER ARTICLES TO READ
Assessors and Appraisers
City Planners
Construction Inspectors
Financial Services Brokers
Property and Real Estate Managers
Real Estate Agents and Brokers

hired, select subcontractors, such as carpenters, to work on the job. Before they break ground, developers may have to satisfy current government regulations.

Developers are ultimately responsible for the success or failure of a project, and they must be knowledgeable concerning every step. They must know how to hire those who can work as part of a team. Developers' careers and reputations are on the line with each project, even if they are not investors who stand to lose money if the project does not go well.

Education and Training

There are no specific educational requirements or certifications for becoming a real estate developer. Many developers have bachelor's or advanced degrees. Most developers enter this career after gaining success in other related fields. Graduate degrees in law, business, and architecture will be of the most help to aspiring developers.

Outlook

The outlook for real estate developers is subject to the fluctuations of the general economy. In the beginning of the 21st century there was slow growth in the real estate industry, and that is expected to continue through the near future, but economic conditions are never fixed. In addition, the real estate market can be quite strong in some parts of the country and weak in others.

For More Information

Read the real estate section of the local newspaper, and follow the building and development activities in your community. A

Fast Fact

Tishman Speyer Properties is one of the largest real estate development companies in the world. Their 2006 sale of 666 5th Avenue in New York City for $1.8 billion was the biggest single-building transaction at that time.

local librarian should be able to refer you to books and magazines about real estate development.

You can gain good experience in certain aspects of real estate development by doing public relations, publicity, or advertising work and participating in fund-raising campaigns for school and community organizations. Volunteering with a housing advocacy organization, such as Habitat for Humanity, may provide opportunities to learn about home construction, bank financing, and legal contracts.

National Association of Industrial & Office Properties
2201 Cooperative Way, Suite 300
Herndon, VA 20171-3034
703-904-7100
http://www.naiop.org

National Association of REALTORS
30700 Russell Ranch Road
Westlake Village, CA 91362-6399
805-557-2300
http://www.realtor.com

Real-Time Captioners

What Real-Time Captioners Do

Real-time captioners, often called *real-time reporters*, create closed captions for live television broadcasts. ("Closed" simply means that the captions may not be seen without special equipment.) Real-time captioners operate a computer-aided transcription (CAT) stenotype system. This is a modified stenotype machine connected to a computer. This computer translates stenographic keystrokes into words.

Captioners type into the steno machine while listening to a live broadcast, transcribing the broadcast accurately while inserting correct punctuation and other symbols. The computer translates the steno strokes into words that are sent electronically to the broadcast site. Within two to three seconds, people across the country can receive the captions on their television screens.

Captioners produce captions for live television programs, such as local and network news broadcasts, talk shows, and sporting events, for the benefit of citizens who are deaf or hard of hearing. The market for captions has expanded, however, to include other groups, such as people learning English as a second language and those learning to read, especially students with reading disabilities. Besides television, captioners work in courtrooms, lawyers' offices, and classrooms.

It takes about one and a half to two hours for a real-time captioner to prepare for an average news broadcast, using preparation materials obtained from the broadcaster and the captioner's own research. Captioners call this pre-show preparation "dictionary-building." They use a wide variety of resources.

Real-time captioners go through resource materials to find words that might come up during a broadcast to develop steno codes that they will use to write these words when they occur during the broadcast.

SCHOOL SUBJECTS
English, Government

MINIMUM EDUCATION LEVEL
Associate's degree

SALARY RANGE
$23,810 to $45,330 to $80,030

OUTLOOK
About as fast as the average

OTHER ARTICLES TO READ
Clerks
Court Reporters
Secretaries
Sign Language Interpreters
Stenographers
Writers

Real-time captioners are extremely proficient in machine shorthand skills and have strong English grammar, spelling, and comprehension skills. Vocabulary skills also are critical to producing accurate captions, particularly at the required speeds of 190 to 250 words per minute.

Education and Training

Typing and computer courses will increase your keyboard speed and accuracy and help you understand word processing programs. Because you will be working with a variety of news, sports, and entertainment programs, you should keep up on current events by taking journalism and government courses.

After high school, you should complete the training to become a court and conference reporter (stenographer), which takes from two to four years. An associate's or bachelor's degree in court and conference reporting, or satisfactory completion of other two-year equivalent programs, is usually required. After graduating from court reporting school, captioners undergo three to six months of on-the-job training.

Outlook

The National Court Reporters Association reports a decline in enrollment in court reporting schools. This may be because of the development of voice and speech systems such as the CAT system, which are computer programs that automatically convert speech to written text. However, there are no current systems that can accurately handle multiple speakers, and it's unlikely that such technology will exist in the near future. Therefore, captioners and court reporters will be in high demand for years to come.

Fast Fact

Gary Robson, a leading captioning professional, runs a Web site that contains a wealth of information about captioning. You can check it out at http://www.robson.org.

With basic real-time skills, captioners will be able to find work in computer-integrated courtrooms; taking real-time depositions for attorneys; providing accompanying litigation support, such as key word indexing; real-timing or captioning in the classroom; or doing broadcast captioning. Other opportunities for the real-time captioner include working with hospitals that specialize in cochlear implants.

For More Information

You can practice transcribing skills by typing taped lectures. Build your vocabulary skills. Learn a foreign language, and increase your awareness of current events, both national and international.

National Captioning Institute
1900 Gallows Road, Suite 3000
Vienna, VA 22182-3874
703-917-7600
http://www.ncicap.org

National Court Reporters Association
8224 Old Courthouse Road
Vienna, VA 22182-3808
800-272-6272
http://www.ncraonline.org

Receptionists

SKILLS SPOTLIGHT
What they do
Communicate ideas
Evaluate and manage information
Manage time

Skills they need
Reading/writing
Responsibility
Speaking/listening

What Receptionists Do

Receptionists are usually the first people to greet clients, patients, or customers when they visit a business. Consequently, the receptionist is responsible for making sure the first impression the caller receives is a good one.

Receptionists' specific responsibilities vary according to where they work. Most greet customers, clients, patients, and salespeople; answer their questions; and direct them to the people in the office they wish to see. Receptionists also answer telephones, take messages for other employees, and receive and distribute mail. In businesses where employees are frequently out of the office on assignments, receptionists may keep track of their whereabouts to ensure they receive important phone calls and messages.

Because they often must answer questions about their place of business, receptionists must know as much as possible about the business's products, services, policies, and practices, and they must be familiar with the names and responsibilities of all employees. Knowing this information is such an important part of a receptionist's job that some businesses call their receptionists *information clerks.*

In some companies, receptionists keep track of other employees' attendance, maintain office security by asking all visitors to sign in and out, and perform clerical duties such as typing, filing, sending and sorting faxes, updating appointment calendars, and simple bookkeeping. Workers in dentists' and physicians' offices admit patients, escort them to examining rooms, schedule appointments, prepare statements, collect bill payments, and answer insurance questions.

Receptionists in hair salons arrange appointments for clients and may escort them to stylists' stations. Workers in bus or train companies answer inquiries about departures, arrivals, and routes. *Registrars, park aides,* and *tourist-information assistants* may be employed as receptionists at public or private facilities. Their duties may include keeping a record of the visitors entering and leaving the facility, as well as providing information on services that the facility provides. Information clerks, *auto-*

SCHOOL SUBJECTS
Business, English

MINIMUM EDUCATION LEVEL
High school diploma

SALARY RANGE
$16,290 to $23,710 to $34,470

OUTLOOK
Faster than the average

OTHER ARTICLES TO READ
Clerks
Customer Service Representatives
Secretaries
Temporary Workers

mobile club information clerks, and *referral-and-information aides* provide answers to questions by telephone or in person from both clients and potential clients and keep a record of all inquiries.

Wherever they work, receptionists must enjoy meeting new people, have a cheery personality, and genuinely want to be helpful.

Education and Training

Employers generally prefer that their receptionists have a high school education, and some businesses prefer to hire workers who have completed postsecondary courses in office administration or management at a junior college or business school. Because most receptionist positions are entry level, however, business or office experience is usually not required.

Outlook

Employment growth for receptionists is expected to be faster than the average through 2016. Many openings will occur due to the occupation's high turnover rate. Opportunities will be best for those with wide clerical skills and work experience.

Because receptionists greet visitors and answer incoming calls, they are often thought of as the face and voice of a company. (Stephen Coburn/Shutterstock)

Growth in jobs for receptionists is expected to be greater than for other clerical positions because automation will have little effect on the receptionist's largely interpersonal duties and because of an anticipated growth in the number of businesses providing services. In addition, more and more businesses are learning how valuable a receptionist can be in furthering their public relations efforts and helping them convey a positive image.

Opportunities should be especially good in rapid services industries, such as physician's offices, law firms, temporary help agencies, and consulting firms.

For More Information

Look for opportunities to interact with the public, answer questions, and provide information, such as hosting special events at school or working at an information desk. Learn basic office skills, such as typing and filing.

American Staffing Association
277 South Washington Street, Suite 200
Alexandria, VA 22314-3675
703-253-2020
asa@americanstaffing.net
http://www.staffingtoday.net

International Association of Administrative Professionals
10502 NW Ambassador Drive
PO Box 20404
Kansas City, MO 64195-0404
816-891-6600
service@iaap-hq.org
http://www.iaap-hq.org

Office & Professional Employees International Union
265 West 14th Street, 6th Floor
New York, NY 10011-7103
800-346-7348
http://www.opeiu.org

Recreational Therapists

What Recreational Therapists Do

Recreational therapists work with people who have mental, physical, or emotional disabilities. They use leisure activities as a form of treatment, much as other health practitioners use surgery, drugs, nutrition, exercise, or psychotherapy.

Recreational therapists consult with doctors, psychiatrists, social workers, physical therapists, and other professionals as well as the patients' families to plan and monitor suitable treatment plans. The recreational therapist needs to understand a patient's ailment, current physical and mental capacities, emotional state, and prospects for recovery and the patient's interests and hobbies.

Some therapists specialize in certain areas. For example, *dance/movement therapists* lead dance and body movement exercises to improve patients' physical and mental well-being. *Art therapists* use drawing, painting, and ceramics as part of their therapeutic and recovery programs. Some therapists work with pets and other animals, such as horses. *Music therapists* conduct solo or group singing, instrumental bands, and rhythm exercises and arrange for patients to listen to live and recorded music. *Horticultural therapists* use gardening and flower arranging activities as therapy.

Recreational therapists plan their programs to meet the needs and capabilities of patients. They carefully monitor and record each patient's progress and report it to the other members of the medical team.

Responsibilities vary depending on the setting in which the recreational therapist works. In nursing homes, the therapist often groups residents according to common or shared interests and ability levels and then plans field trips, parties, entertainment, and other group activities. A therapist in a community center might work in a day care program for the elderly or

SCHOOL SUBJECTS
Biology, Psychology
MINIMUM EDUCATION LEVEL
Bachelor's degree
SALARY RANGE
$21,700 to $36,940 to $58,030
OUTLOOK
More slowly than the average

OTHER ARTICLES TO READ
Creative Arts Therapists
Human Services Workers
Kinesiologists
Occupational Therapists
Physical Therapists
Recreation Workers
Rehabilitation Counselors
Sports Coaches

A recreational therapist (r) helps her patient use a Wii baseball game as part of his therapy. This type of game helps the patient with his balance and coordination. (Getty Images)

in a program for mentally disabled adults. Recreational therapists in community settings may have to arrange transportation and escort services for prospective participants. Developing therapeutic recreation programs in community settings requires a large measure of organizational ability, flexibility, and ingenuity.

Recreational therapists must enjoy and be enthusiastic about the activities in which they involve their clients. They also need patience and a positive attitude.

Education and Training

To be a recreational therapist, you need at least a bachelor's degree. Acceptable majors are recreational therapy, therapeutic recreation, and recreation with a concentration in therapeutic recreation. You will also have to complete a supervised internship or field placement lasting about three months. Advanced degrees are recommended for therapists who want to advance to supervisory, administrative, and teaching positions.

Licensing for recreational therapists is required in some states, and professional certification is required in others. Some states and facilities regulate the use of the title Recreational Therapist. Many hospitals and other employers require certification.

Outlook

Employment growth for recreational therapists will be slower than the average through 2016. Employment will decline slightly in hospitals and nursing homes, but faster employment growth is expected in assisted living, outpatient physical and psychiatric rehabilitation, and services for people with disabilities.

For More Information

Volunteering in a nursing home, hospital, or care facility for adults with disabilities is a good way to learn about the daily realities of institutional living. Also check for volunteer opportunities at community centers that have recreational programs for people with disabilities.

American Therapeutic Recreation Association
207 3rd Avenue
Hattiesburg, MS 39401-3688
601-450-2872
http://www.atra-tr.org

National Council for Therapeutic Recreation Certification
7 Elmwood Drive
New City, NY 10956-5136
845-639-1439
http://www.nctrc.org

National Therapeutic Recreation Society/ National Recreation and Park Association
22377 Belmont Ridge Road
Ashburn, VA 20148-4501
703-858-0784
http://www.nrpa.org

# Recreation Workers

SKILLS SPOTLIGHT

What they do
Communicate ideas
Help clients and customers
Teach

Skills they need
Creative thinking
Social
Speaking/listening

What Recreation Workers Do

Recreation workers help people make the most of their free time by planning, organizing, and directing leisure activities. They often work for local government and volunteer agencies, planning programs at community centers, neighborhood playgrounds, prisons, and hospitals.

Recreation workers organize programs that include arts and crafts, dramatics, music and dancing, swimming, camping, and nature study. Special events include pet and hobby shows, contests, and festivals. Workers may plan activities for people with special needs, such as the elderly or people with disabilities.

Recreation center directors run programs at day camps, playgrounds, or recreation buildings. They direct the staffs and make sure the buildings and equipment are safe and well maintained. *Recreation leaders*, along with their *assistants*, work directly with participants. Leaders help train volun-

teers. In industry, recreation leaders plan social and athletic programs for employees and their families. Bowling leagues, softball teams, picnics, and dances are examples of company-sponsored activities. In addition, an increasing number of companies are providing exercise and fitness programs for their employees.

Camp counselors lead and teach both children and adults such skills as swimming, hiking, horseback riding, and other outdoor sports and games as well as give instruction in nature and folklore. Camp counselors teach skills such as wood crafting, leather working, and basket weaving. Some camps offer specialized instruction in subjects such as music, drama, gymnastics, and computers.

Another type of recreation worker is the *social director*, who plans and organizes activities for guests in hotels and resorts or for passengers on ships. Social directors greet guests, explain the programs available, and try to encourage people to participate in activities such as card parties, games, contests, dances, musicals, or field trips. They

SCHOOL SUBJECTS
Physical education, Theater/Dance

MINIMUM EDUCATION LEVEL
High school diploma

SALARY RANGE
$14,980 to $21,220 to $36,730

OUTLOOK
Faster than the average

OTHER ARTICLES TO READ
Amusement Park Workers
Cruise Ship Workers
Lifeguards and Swimming Instructors
Recreational Therapists
Resort Workers
Ski Resort Workers

Fast Fact

may be required to set up equipment, arrange for transportation, or plan decorations, refreshments, or entertainment.

Cruise directors plan daily activities and entertainment for passengers. *Ski resort workers* operate ski lifts, teach skiing lessons, patrol ski trails, and direct the operation of ski lodges.

Education and Training

For some recreation jobs a high school diploma is enough preparation, but for most full-time jobs in parks and recreation or in social work, you need a college degree. Acceptable college majors include parks and recreation management, leisure studies, fitness management, and related disciplines. For some positions you need special training in a field such as art, music, drama, or sports.

Outlook

Job opportunities for recreation workers are expected to increase faster than the average through 2016. Growth in the recreation field will result from a continuing interest in fitness and health and a growing elderly population in nursing homes and retirement communities. There also is a demand for recreation workers to conduct activity programs for special-needs groups.

Two areas promising the most favorable opportunities for recreation workers are the commercial recreation and social service industries. Commercial recreation establishments include amusement parks, sports and entertainment centers, wilderness and survival enterprises, tourist attractions, vacation excursions, hotels and other resorts, camps, health spas, athletic clubs, and apartment complexes. Social service agencies include senior centers, halfway houses, children's homes, and day care programs for the mentally or developmentally disabled.

For More Information

Volunteer to work in recreation programs at nursing homes, community centers, and camps. Participate in a variety of recreation activities, including sports, games, arts and crafts, music, dance, and nature study.

American Alliance for Health, Physical Education, Recreation & Dance
1900 Association Dr.
Reston, VA 20191-1598
800-213-7193, ext. 430
http://www.aahperd.org/aalr

American Camping Association
5000 State Road 67 North
Martinsville, IN 46151-7902
765-342-8456
http://www.acacamps.org

National Recreation and Park Association
22377 Belmont Ridge Road
Ashburn, VA 20148-4501
703-858-0784
info@nrpa.org
http://www.nrpa.org

Recycling Coordinators

What Recycling Coordinators Do

Recycling coordinators manage a town's or city's recycling program. They make sure city workers or private contractors are collecting, sorting, and processing recyclable materials. They also may help find new markets for recyclables, manage a staff, and report to local authorities. Some coordinators promote recycling programs in their communities.

In the mid-1960s garbage was piling up in a lot of major cities, and authorities were not doing a good job of managing the trash. In an effort to solve this problem, federal and state laws established new requirements for handling municipal solid waste (MSW). Today, most U.S. municipalities want to keep as much MSW out of landfills and incinerators as possible. Landfills are places where waste is buried. They can leak hazardous substances into surrounding land and release toxic

emissions. Incinerators are used to burn trash, and they, too, can release toxic emissions. When more trash is recycled, less has to be burned or buried.

Each recycling program differs according to the community, location, population, funding, and other factors. Source reduction is part of many of these plans. This means discouraging people from throwing out a lot of trash in the first place. Some cities pick up just one bag of trash per household per week and charge a fee for more bags. Other communities limit or ban disposal of certain wastes. To collect recyclables, some communities have drop-off points where residents can bring paper, glass, aluminum, or other materials. Others ask people to put recyclables in special bags and throw them out with the rest of the trash. Paper, glass, and aluminum are the materials most often recycled. Other materials that can be recycled include animal waste, yard waste, appliances, wood wastes (such as shipping

SCHOOL SUBJECTS
Business, Earth science

MINIMUM EDUCATION LEVEL
Bachelor's degree

SALARY RANGE
$25,090 to $39,370 to $63,670

OUTLOOK
About as fast as the average

OTHER ARTICLES TO READ
Ecologists
Environmental Technicians
Hazardous Waste Management Technicians
Refuse Collectors
Soil Conservation Technicians
Wastewater Treatment Plant Operators
  and Technicians

pallets and boxes), motor oil, scrap metal, plastic drink bottles, and tires.

Recycling coordinators are in charge of educating the public about the recycling programs that are available in their communities. They encourage people to recycle by keeping them informed of what materials can be recycled, how they should be packaged, and where and when to deposit them.

Education and Training

To prepare for this career, it is recommended that you focus your studies on business, economics, English, math, and science.

A bachelor's degree in environmental studies or a related area plus business experience and proven communication skills is desirable. Some colleges and universities are developing a minor in integrated waste management. Classes include public policy, source reduction, transformation technology (composting/waste energy), and landfills.

Outlook

Employment for municipal recycling coordinators is expected to grow about as fast as the average through 2016. As states try to meet their waste-reduction and recycling goals, people who can make it happen on the local level are going to be in demand.

Nationwide, the waste management and recycling industries will need more people to run recovery facilities, design new recycling technologies, come up with

A recycling coordinator leads a tour through a recycling facility for a group of elementary school students. (Getty Images)

new ways to use recyclables, and do related work. Private businesses are also expected to hire recycling coordinators to manage in-house programs.

For More Information

Learn about the recycling issues in your community and state. Volunteer to help with fund drives and information campaigns for a recycling organization.

Environmental Careers Organization
http://www.eco.org

National Recycling Coalition
805 15th Street, NW, Suite 425
Washington, DC 20005-2239
202-789-1430
info@nrc-recycle.org
http://www.nrc-recycle.org

Reflexologists

What Reflexologists Do

Reflexologists believe that the feet and hands provide a kind of map to the rest of the body. They believe that certain spots on the feet and hands, called reflexes, are connected to certain spots on other parts of the body. They apply pressure to these reflexes so that they can affect the parts of the body that are connected to the reflexes. A reflexologist uses special methods to work on all the parts of the feet or hands, paying special attention to sore spots. A sore spot means that there is a problem in the part of the body that is connected to that spot on the foot or hand. Reflexologists believe that their special kind of massage can improve circulation, help people heal more quickly when they are sick, and help people relax.

Some reflexologists work on hands, but most work on feet. Every foot has more than 7,000 nerve endings, and those nerve endings are close to the surface of the foot. That is why feet are so sensitive. Also, since feet are larger than hands, it is easier to find the reflexes on feet.

Reflexologists believe that their treatments help keep the energy flowing throughout the body. They also believe that their treatments reduce the amount of lactic acid in the feet. Lactic acid is a natural waste product that the body generates, and too much of it is unhealthy. Reflexologists also believe that their treatments break up calcium crystals that have built up in the nerve endings of the feet. It has never been proved that reflexology works in these ways. Most scientists do not believe that the theories that reflexology is based on are correct, but even some of those scientists enjoy reflexology treatments.

Some people try reflexology because they hope that it can solve a particular health problem that they have, but many people go for treatments simply because reflexology makes them feel good. Many people try reflexology when traditional medicine has failed to solve their health problems.

SCHOOL SUBJECTS
Biology, Health
MINIMUM EDUCATION LEVEL
Some postsecondary training
SALARY RANGE
$32,530 to $65,890 to $97,880
OUTLOOK
Faster than the average

OTHER ARTICLES TO READ
Aromatherapists
Chiropractors
Kinesiologists
Massage Therapists
Myotherapists
Oriental Medicine Practitioners

Education and Training

Anyone who wants to become a reflexologist should know as much about medicine and health as possible. Important school subjects are biology, chemistry, and health. Psychology may also be useful. Learn as much as you can about alternative medicine and bodywork.

The most important part of a reflexologist's training involves completing a comprehensive course of study and becoming certified by a reputable school. One of the best courses is conducted by the International Institute of Reflexology.

In most states, reflexologists are subject to the laws that govern massage therapists. That may mean that you must complete a state-certified course in massage before being licensed to practice reflexology.

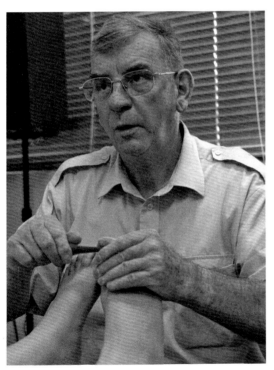

Reflexologists work with the pressure points on the feet to bring about overall health changes. (AFP/Getty Images)

Outlook

The field of reflexology is expanding much more rapidly than the average for all fields. Although science still views it with skepticism, reflexology has become popular in a short period of time. It also has benefited from the popular acceptance of alternative medicine and therapies in recent years, particularly because it is a holistic practice that aims to treat the whole person rather than the symptoms of disease or discomfort. Because reflexology treatments involve little risk to the client in most cases, they provide a safe and convenient way to improve health.

For More Information

Read as much as you can about reflexology. Many books are currently available, and many more will be available in the near future, since the field is growing rapidly. Learn as much as you can about other alternative therapies, especially other forms of massage such as shiatsu or myotherapy.

American Massage Therapy Association
500 Davis Street, Suite 900
Evanston, IL 60201-4615
877-905-2700
info@amtamassage.org
http://www.amtamassage.org

American Reflexology Certification Board
PO Box 5147
Gulfport, FL 33737-5147
303-933-6921
http://www.arcb.net

The International Institute of Reflexology
5650 First Avenue North
PO Box 12642
St. Petersburg, FL 33733-2642
727-343-4811
iir@reflexology-usa.net
http://www.reflexology-usa.net

Refuse Collectors

SKILLS SPOTLIGHT
What they do
Exercise leadership
Help clients and customers
Work with a team

Skills they need
Responsibility
Self-management
Speaking/listening

What Refuse Collectors Do

Refuse collectors pick up garbage and other waste materials from homes, businesses, and industries and transport it in trucks to landfills or giant incinerators for disposal or burning.

Depending on local requirements, the refuse may be loose in containers, in packaging such as plastic bags, in preapproved containers that indicate recyclable materials, or, for newspapers and magazines, tied in bundles. When the truck is full, the workers drive with the load to the disposal site and empty the truck. Workers also may pick up cast-off furniture, old appliances, or other large, bulky items.

An average day for refuse collectors often begins before dawn with an inspection of the truck that includes checking lights and tires, testing air and oil pressure gauges, and making sure a spill kit is on board. Refuse collectors who work on commercial routes or pick up dumpsters stay in contact with dispatchers via radio or cellular phone to receive pick-up locations. Refuse collectors gas up their trucks as needed and recheck the truck's vital equipment at the end of the day.

Sometimes work duties are divided among the workers, with the driver doing only the driving all day long. In other cases, the workers alternate between driving and loading and unloading throughout the day. Some refuse collectors work alone, and they are responsible for driving the truck and loading the refuse.

Refuse workers must work outdoors in all kinds of weather, including cold, snow, rain, and heat, and they must handle dirty, smelly objects. The work is often strenuous, requiring the lifting of heavy refuse containers, hopping on and off the truck constantly, and operating hoists and other equipment. Because there is a danger of infection from raw garbage, they must wear protective gloves and are sometimes pro-

SCHOOL SUBJECTS	
Physical education, Technical/Shop	
MINIMUM EDUCATION LEVEL	
High school diploma	
SALARY RANGE	
$17,070 to $29,420 to $50,320	
OUTLOOK	
More slowly than the average	

OTHER ARTICLES TO READ
Ecologists
Environmental Technicians
Hazardous Waste Management Technicians
Recycling Coordinators
Soil Conservation Technicians
Wastewater Treatment Plant Operators
    and Technicians

vided with uniforms. Most workers wear heavy steel-toe boots to help avoid foot injuries from accidentally dropping containers or large objects.

Education and Training

Although it is not absolutely necessary, many refuse collection companies prefer that their employees be high school graduates. Most employers require workers to be at least 18 years old. Auto mechanics and other shop courses, English, and mathematics are recommended. New employees receive on-the-job training in addition to instruction on safety precautions.

Workers who drive collection trucks need a commercial driver's license (CDL). In some areas where the workers alternate jobs, a CDL is required even of those who are generally loaders. A clean driving record is a necessity. Refuse collectors may have to pass a civil service test to work for a city or town.

Outlook

Employment growth for refuse collectors is expected to be slower than the average through 2016, but job turnover is high in this field. Every year, many positions will become available as workers transfer to other jobs or leave the workforce.

Opportunities will be best in heavily populated regions in and near big cities, where the most waste is generated. In cities, increasing use of mechanized equipment for lifting and emptying large refuse containers may decrease the need for refuse collectors. However, as communities encourage more recycling and more resource recovery technologies, job availability may stabilize.

Refuse collectors make regular pickups of garbage and recycling and are an important part of keeping cities clean. (Vadim Kozlovsky/Shutterstock)

For More Information

Volunteer to work at community recycling centers. Since physical strength is a requirement for this job, you might participate in activities that increase your endurance, such as weight lifting or body building.

Environmental Industry Association
4301 Connecticut Avenue, NW, Suite 300
Washington, DC 20008-2304
202-244-4700
http://www.envasns.org

International Brotherhood of Teamsters
25 Louisiana Avenue NW
Washington, DC 20001-2130
202-624-6800
http://www.teamster.org

National Solid Wastes Management Association
4301 Connecticut Avenue, NW, Suite 300
Washington, DC 20008-2304
202-244-4700
http://www.nswma.org

Rehabilitation Counselors

What Rehabilitation Counselors Do

Rehabilitation counselors provide counseling and guidance services to people with disabilities. The counselor helps them train for and locate work that is suitable to their physical and mental abilities, interests, and aptitudes. The rehabilitation counselor identifies the client's specific difficulties and develops a plan of action to remove or reduce the barriers the client faces.

Clients are referred to rehabilitation programs from physicians, hospitals, social workers, employment agencies, schools, or accident commissions. An employer may also seek help for an individual. Sometimes people seek help on their own, and sometimes their families bring them in.

The counselor's first step is to determine the nature and extent of the disability and evaluate how that disability interferes with work and other life functions. This determination is made from medical and psychological reports as well as from family history, educational background, work experience, and other information. The next step is to determine a vocational direction and plan of services to overcome the handicaps to employment or independent living.

The rehabilitation counselor coordinates a comprehensive evaluation of a client's physical functioning abilities and vocational interests, aptitudes, and skills. This information is used to develop a vocational or independent-living goal for the client and to determine the services or training necessary to reach that goal. Services that the rehabilitation counselor may coordinate or provide include physical and mental restoration, academic or vocational training, vocational counseling, job analysis, job modification or reasonable accommodation, and job placement. Limited financial assistance in the form of maintenance or transportation assistance may also be provided.

Growth Field

Between 2006 and 2016 the number of rehabilitation counselors is expected to grow from 141,000 to 173,000, an increase of about 23 percent.

Education and Training

If you are interested in a career as a rehabilitation counselor, take psychology, sociology, English, biology, and college preparatory courses.

A master's degree in rehabilitation counseling, counseling and guidance, or counseling psychology is preferred for those entering the field. Some positions as aides are available for people with bachelor's degrees in rehabilitation counseling. Preparation for a master's degree program requires an undergraduate major in behavioral sciences, social sciences, or a related field, or the completion of an undergraduate degree program in rehabilitation counseling. Certification, licensing, or registration is required for counselors in 46 states.

Outlook

The passage of the Americans with Disabilities Act of 1990 has increased the demand for rehabilitation counselors. Budget pressures may serve to limit the number of new rehabilitation counselors to be hired by government agencies; however, the overall outlook remains excellent.

Employment growth for all counselors is expected to be faster than the average through 2016. Some of this growth can be attributed to the advances in medical technology that are saving more lives. In addition, more employers are offering employee assistance programs that provide mental health and alcohol and drug abuse services.

For More Information

Look for opportunities to volunteer at nursing homes, children's camps for disabled youngsters, or rehabilitation agencies. Other possibilities include reading for the blind or tutoring young children who have disabilities.

American Rehabilitation Counseling Association
PO Box 791006
Baltimore, MD 21279-1006
800-347-6647
http://www.arcaweb.org

National Rehabilitation Association
633 South Washington Street
Alexandria, VA 22314-4109
703-836-0850
info@nationalrehab.org
http://www.nationalrehab.org

National Rehabilitation Counseling Association
PO Box 4480
Manassas, VA 20108-4480
703-361-2077
info@nrca-net.org
http://nrca-net.org

Religious Sisters and Brothers

What Religious Sisters and Brothers Do

In the Roman Catholic Church, the titles "sister" and "brother" are given to members of religious communities. *Religious sisters and brothers* take vows of poverty, chastity, and obedience and devote their lives to God. Sisters and brothers generally view their way of life not so much as a career but as a vocation or calling. *Active religious sisters and brothers* are distinct from *contemplative religious sisters and brothers.*

Active religious sisters and brothers are engaged in education, health care, social work, and spreading the Catholic faith, either as missionaries or through their daily work. Sisters and brothers may work at the elementary, high school, or college level, usually in Catholic-funded schools. Others serve as librarians, counselors, or principals. Some active sisters and brothers work in hospitals or medical centers as nurses, physicians, pharmacists, medical technicians, administrators, or physical therapists.

In impoverished areas, such as migrant worker camps and inner cities, active religious sisters and brothers may live among the people, teaching basic literacy and life skills such as sanitary procedures and job skills. Those involved in social work may conduct programs to help the poor or homeless or work in homes for disadvantaged children. Sisters and brothers who work as missionaries may work in countries plagued by famine, disease, war or civil strife, or places where the Catholic faith has not yet been established. At the heart of all this activity is the desire to love and serve God.

Contemplative sisters and brothers devote themselves entirely to private prayer and the celebration of the mass and the Liturgy of the Hours. Cloistered contemplative religious sisters and brothers live apart from the rest of the world in monasteries and convents. Contemplative brothers are often called *monks*, while contemplative sisters are called *nuns*.

SCHOOL SUBJECTS
English, History, Religion

MINIMUM EDUCATION LEVEL
High school diploma

SALARY RANGE
$15,420 to $26,660 to $54,120

OUTLOOK
Much faster than the average

OTHER ARTICLES TO READ
College Professors
Elementary School Teachers
Roman Catholic Priests
School Administrators
Secondary School Teachers
Social Workers

Education and Training

Contemplative religious sisters and brothers believe that they are called by God to dedicate their lives to service of the church, and their religious communities must feel certain that aspiring members are called. All sisters and brothers must take the traditional vows of poverty, chastity, and obedience.

If you are interested in becoming a religious sister or brother, you should enroll, if possible, in a Catholic high school. You should take courses in religion, English, and speech.

Many religious orders advise applicants to attend college because they want prospective members to have life experience before becoming a sister or brother. Sisters and brothers often are trained for their service work by the order or congregation in which they take their vows. Training programs commonly last several years.

Outlook

Opportunities for religious sisters and brothers are practically unlimited, for two major reasons. The first is that the Catholic Church wholeheartedly encourages those who have been called to live a life completely devoted to serving God. The

Some nuns work as nurses in hospitals. (photobank ch/Shutterstock)

second reason for the great opportunities in religious life is the decline in vocations over the past few decades. A majority of today's sisters and brothers are more than 50 years old.

For More Information

Get in touch with a religious community that interests you, either directly or through your priest. Some religious orders offer special retreats or similar programs to help potential sisters and brothers discern their vocation. Volunteer to work at Catholic Church-sponsored hospitals, religious education classes, or social service agencies. Attend mass and other services frequently; read about church history, doctrine, and current events; take part in parish activities.

Daughters of St. Paul
4403 Veterans Memorial Boulevard
Metairie, LA 70006-5321
504-887-7635
http://www.pauline.org

National Religious Vocation Conference
5401 South Cornell Avenue, Suite 207
Chicago, IL 60615-5664
773-363-5454
http://www.nrvc.net

Order of Preachers (Dominicans)
http://www.op.org

Province of St. Mary Capuchin Franciscans
30 Gedney Park Drive
White Plains, NY 10605-3534
914-761-3008
http://www.capuchin.net

School Sisters of Notre Dame
13105 Watertown Plank Road
Elm Grove, WI 53122-2291
communications@ssnd.org
http://www.ssnd.org

Renewable Energy Workers

What Renewable Energy Workers Do

Renewable energy is power or fuel that comes from wind, sunlight (solar), water (hydro), organic matter (biomass), and the Earth's internal heat (geothermal).

Wind energy is generated by wind turbines. Wind plants, or wind farms, have many of these turbines, which can generate electricity for tens of thousands of homes. *Electrical, mechanical, and aeronautical engineers* design and test the turbines as well as the wind farms. *Meteorologists* help identify prime locations for new project sites and serve as consultants on projects. *Skilled construction workers* build the farms; *windsmiths*, sometimes called *mechanical or electrical technicians*, operate and maintain the turbines and other equipment.

The most common solar energy technology today uses photovoltaic (PV) cells, which absorb sunlight and turn it into electricity. *Electrical, mechanical, and chemical engineers* work in research and development departments. *Architects*, many of whom specialize in passive solar design and construction, design solar-powered structures. *Technicians, electricians, installers, and construction workers* build and maintain solar projects.

Hydropower uses the energy of flowing water to produce electricity. Electrical and mechanical engineers and technicians design, construct, and maintain hydropower projects. *Biologists and other environmental scientists* assess the effects of hydropower projects on wildlife and the environment. *Recreation managers* and *trail planners* manage and preserve the land surrounding reservoirs or dams.

Bioenergy is the energy stored in biomass—organic matter such as trees, straw, or corn. *Chemists, biochemists, biologists, and agricultural scientists* work together to find faster and less costly ways to produce bioenergy. *Engineers, construction workers, electricians*, and *technicians* build and maintain bioenergy conversion plants. *Farmers*

SCHOOL SUBJECTS
Biology, Physics
MINIMUM EDUCATION LEVEL
Varies according to position
SALARY RANGE
$25,360 to $40,690 to $67,590
OUTLOOK
Varies according to industry

OTHER ARTICLES TO READ
Agricultural Engineers
Architects
Electrical and Electronics Engineers
Environmental Engineers
Geophysicists
Meteorologists

and *foresters* raise and harvest crops or other sources of biomass.

Geothermal heat comes from the heat within the earth. Water heated from geothermal energy is tapped from its underground reservoirs and used to heat buildings, grow crops, or melt snow, and to generate electricity. The geothermal industry employs *geologists*, *geochemists*, and *geophysicists* to research and locate new reservoirs. *Hydraulic engineers*, *reservoir engineers*, and *drillers* work together to reach and maintain the reservoir's heat supply.

Education and Training

A strong background in science and mathematics is necessary for many jobs in the renewable energy industry. Most technical jobs require at least an associate's or bachelor's degree.

Outlook

The wind industry is the fastest-growing sector of the renewable energy industry, and rapid growth is expected in the next decade, especially for windsmiths, engineers, meteorologists, electricians, and other technical workers.

Solar energy use is already well established in high-value markets such as remote power, satellites, and communications. The manufacturing of PV cell systems will present many employment opportunities.

Growth in the hydropower industry will be limited by the fact that most potential sites for hydropower projects have already been tapped.

Fast Fact

Renewable energy sources are used to produce approximately 2 percent of all electricity in the United States, according to the National Energy Policy Development Group (NEPDG).

Bioenergy is experiencing steady growth, with good employment opportunities for chemists, engineers, and other agricultural scientists. Employment opportunities in geothermal energy are greatest in the West for the drilling of geothermal energy, and in the Midwest for geothermal heat pumps.

For More Information

Many professional associations have student chapters or junior clubs.

Energy Efficiency and Renewable Energy Clearinghouse
U.S. Department of Energy
Mail Stop EE-1
Washington, DC 20585-0001
877-337-3463
http://www.eere.energy.gov

National Renewable Energy Laboratory
U.S. Department of Energy
1617 Cole Boulevard
Golden, CO 80401-3393
http://www.nrel.gov

Reporters

SKILLS SPOTLIGHT
What they do
Communicate ideas
Evaluate and manage information
Teach

Skills they need
Creative thinking
Reading/writing
Speaking/listening

What Reporters Do

Reporters gather information and report the news for radio, television, magazines, newspapers, and the Internet. They cover stories on local, national, or international events. News stories may be a one-day item, such as a power failure or weather-related piece. Or reporters may cover a period of days or weeks on subjects such as trials, investigations, major disasters, and government issues. *Correspondents* cover stories from a specific area. For example, each national network station has a White House correspondent, a Congressional correspondent, and a Pentagon correspondent.

To gather information, reporters take notes and record or videotape interviews with news sources. Reporters also examine documents related to the story. Before reporters start putting together their stories, they discuss the importance of the subject matter with a newspaper editor or a producer. Editors and producers decide what news will be covered each day.

Reporters then organize the information and write a concise, informative story. Reporters and correspondents who are too far from their editorial office to return to file their reports may phone, e-mail, or fax.

Because of continual deadline pressure, a reporter's life is hectic. Stories for nightly news broadcasts have to be in and reviewed by the producer before airtime. Newspaper articles must be filed long before the first edition is printed, which is usually in the very early hours of the morning. If a major news story takes place, reporters may have to work 18 or 20 hours without a break.

Some correspondents are assigned to cover dangerous areas. War stories are frequently filed from the country in which the war is taking place. Reporters who cover riots, floods, major disasters, and other

SCHOOL SUBJECTS
English, Journalism

MINIMUM EDUCATION LEVEL
Bachelor's degree

SALARY RANGE
$19,440 to $34,690 to $76,230

OUTLOOK
More slowly than the average

OTHER ARTICLES TO READ
Foreign Correspondents
Magazine Editors
Music Journalists
Newspaper Editors
Photojournalists
Political Columnists and Writers
Political Reporters
Radio and Television Announcers
Science and Medical Writers
Sportswriters
Writers

stories must be able to work in difficult, dangerous, and upsetting situations.

Education and Training

You can begin to prepare for a career as a reporter in school by taking courses in English, writing, history, typing, and computer science.

After high school, you should go to college and earn a bachelor's degree. Your degree can be in journalism or liberal arts.

Journalism courses and programs are also offered by many community and junior colleges, but graduates of these programs may have trouble competing with people who have more education. Master's degrees are becoming more important for journalists, particularly for teachers and specialists.

If you plan to specialize in a particular subject, such as science writing, it is important to take several courses in that subject.

Outlook

Employment growth for reporters and correspondents through 2016 is expected to be slower than the average. Newspaper jobs are expected to decrease because of

Television reporters may film their stories out in the field or inside the television studio. (Joseph Dilag/Shutterstock)

mergers, consolidations, and closures in the newspaper industry. Because of an increase in the number of small community and suburban daily and weekly newspapers, opportunities will be best for journalism graduates who are willing to relocate and accept relatively low starting salaries.

A significant number of jobs will be provided by magazines and in radio and television broadcasting, but the major news magazines and larger broadcasting stations generally prefer experienced reporters. Some employment growth is expected for reporters in online newspapers and magazines.

For More Information

Work on your school newspaper or on your religious center's newsletter. You can offer to be a reporter or writer, or you can help with word processing and printing. Read your local newspaper regularly. Follow the work of one or two reporters who cover a topic that interests you, such as politics, science, or culture.

Association for Education in Journalism & Mass Communication
234 Outlet Pointe Boulevard
Columbia, SC 29210-5667
803-798-0271
http://www.aejmc.org

Newspaper Association of America
4401 Wilson Boulevard, Suite 900
Arlington, VA 22203-1867
571-366-1000
http://www.naa.org

Radio-Television News Directors Association
1025 F Street, NW, 7th Floor
Washington, DC 20004-1412
202-659-6510
http://www.rtnda.org

Research Assistants

What Research Assistants Do

Research assistants help find facts, information, and statistics. They work for scientists, editors and writers, publishers, filmmakers, attorneys, and advertising executives, among others. Today, almost every field imaginable hires research assistants to help get jobs done more thoroughly and quickly.

After they receive an assignment, research assistants decide how to find information. They may spend hours, days, or even weeks of research in archives, libraries, laboratories, museums, on the Internet, or talking to experts. They write up notes or a report of the information.

Research assistants who work for writers or editors help find statistics or other information for a specific article or book. Some research assistants called *fact checkers* make sure that facts, such as dates, ages, and numbers, are correct before they are published. Research assistants who work in radio, film, and television might help to find and verify historical information or locate experts to be interviewed. Those who work in the sciences, engineering, or medicine help scientists find background information for their experiments.

University professors hire research assistants, often graduate students, to help them in their research. For example, a history professor working on a paper about the Italian military might send a research assistant to the library to find facts about the Italian military presence in Greece during World War II.

Advertising agencies and marketing departments hire research assistants to help them decide how and when a product should be sold. Law firms hire research assistants to find out facts about past cases and laws. Politicians hire research assistants to help find out how a campaign is succeeding or failing, to find statistics on outcomes of past elections, and to determine the issues that are especially important to the constituents.

SCHOOL SUBJECTS
English, History

MINIMUM EDUCATION LEVEL
Bachelor's degree

SALARY RANGE
$26,750 to $37,350 to $61,080

OUTLOOK
About as fast as the average

OTHER ARTICLES TO READ
Congressional Aides
Demographers
Historians
Information Brokers
Marketing Researchers
Public Opinion Researchers
Reporters

As a result of technological advancements, a new career niche has developed for *information brokers*, who compile information from online databases and services.

Education and Training

History, English, mathematics, and foreign language classes are good preparation for this career. Pay special attention to your writing and research skills. If you are interested in science and engineering research, you should take all the laboratory courses you can.

Education requirements vary, depending on the field in which you work. Most employers require an undergraduate degree. Some fields, especially the sciences, engineering, and law, may require you to have an advanced degree or other special training.

Fast Fact

The Internet can be a valuable resource in starting a research project, because it can help you figure out the direction your research may take. Search engines such as Google give you an idea of what sources are available, and a good encyclopedia site like Britannica.com can help you check facts.

Outlook

The outlook for the research assistant career generally depends on the field in which the researcher works. A researcher with a good background in many fields will be in higher demand, as will a researcher with specialized knowledge and research techniques specific to a field.

Research assistants with good experience, excellent work ethics, and the drive to succeed will rarely find themselves out of work.

For More Information

School assignments provide opportunities to experiment with different types of research. Ask a resource librarian to teach you about the many research tools available in a library. Work as a reporter for your school newspaper, or volunteer to write feature articles for your yearbook.

National Institutes of Health
9000 Rockville Pike
Bethesda, Maryland 20892-0001
http://ohrm.cc.nih.gov

The University of Pennsylvania College of Arts and Sciences
120 Claudia Cohen Hall
249 South 36th Street
Philadelphia, PA 19104-6304
215-898-6341
http://www.college.upenn.edu

U.S. Census Bureau
4600 Silver Hill Road
Washington, DC 20233-0001
301-763-4748
recruiter@census.gov
http://www.census.gov

Reservation and Ticket Agents

What Reservation and Ticket Agents Do

Reservation and ticket agents make and confirm travel arrangements for clients and prepare and sell tickets to customers. They help travelers plan their trips by answering questions about trip prices. They suggest what routes to take and when to begin and end a journey.

Reservation agents usually work in large offices answering telephone calls from customers and booking reservations. Most agents work for airlines, but the same procedures are followed by agents who work for bus, train, or other transportation companies. After they find out when and where the customer wants to go, reservation agents type instructions on a computer keyboard and quickly obtain information on flight, bus, or train schedules. If a plane is full, the agents may suggest an alternate flight or check to see if space is available on another airline that flies to the same location.

Ticket agents sell tickets to customers at airports, bus terminals, and railway stations. They answer customer questions and may check baggage, examine visas or passports (if the passenger is traveling to a foreign country), ensure passenger seating, and direct passengers to the proper boarding areas. Ticket agents also keep records of the passengers departing on each trip.

When flights or train or bus runs are delayed or canceled because of poor weather or other conditions, reservation and ticket agents must explain the situation to unhappy travelers and try to make other arrangements for them. Because the transportation industry operates 24 hours a day, reservation and ticket agents often work irregular hours, including evenings and weekends.

Reservation and ticket agents should be able to read and understand travel schedules and have some computer skills. Agents

SCHOOL SUBJECTS
Business, English
MINIMUM EDUCATION LEVEL
High school diploma
SALARY RANGE
$18,290 to $29,820 to $46,670
OUTLOOK
About as fast as the average

OTHER ARTICLES TO READ
Clerks
Customer Service Representatives
Flight Attendants
Receptionists
Retail Sales Workers
Secretaries
Travel Agents

who speak a foreign language are always in great demand, as more and more international travel occurs each year.

Education and Training

Although there are no specific educational requirements to become a reservation or ticket agent, most employers prefer to hire high school graduates with at least some college training. As the field becomes more competitive, a college degree will become increasingly important.

All agents receive some classroom instruction and on-the-job training, during which they are taught how to read schedules, calculate fares, and make travel arrangements.

Outlook

Employment growth for reservation and ticket agents is expected to be about as fast as the average for all occupations through 2016. Ticketless travel, or automated reservations ticketing, is reducing the need for agents. In addition, many airports now have computerized kiosks that allow passengers to reserve and purchase tickets themselves. Passengers can also access information about fares and flight times on the Internet, where they can also make reservations and purchase tickets. However, for security reasons, all of these services cannot be fully automated, so the need for reservation and transportation ticket agents will never be completely eliminated.

Most openings will occur as experienced agents transfer to other occupations or retire. Competition for jobs is fierce due to declining demand and low turnover, and because of the glamour and attractive travel benefits associated with the industry.

For More Information

Ask your parents to let you help plan your next family vacation. You can help choose a location that interests all members of your family and assemble information about the location you plan to visit. Check libraries and Web sites. Send for brochures, maps, and other information from a city, state, or country's tourism office. Help figure out the best way to travel to your vacation spot. Use the Internet or the telephone to contact air, bus, and rail lines to find out prices and schedules.

Tourism Cares for Tomorrow
275 Turnpike Street, Suite 307
Canton, MA 02021-2357
781-821-5990
http://www.ntfonline.org

Travel Industry Association of America
1100 New York Avenue, NW, Suite 450
Washington, DC 20005-3934
202-408-8422
http://www.tia.org

World Tourism Organization
Capitán Haya 42
28020 Madrid, Spain
+34 91 567 81 00
omt@unwto.org
http://www.unwto.org

Reservation and ticket agents should be courteous and helpful to their customers. (Getty Images)

Resort Workers

SKILLS SPOTLIGHT
What they do
Communicate ideas
Exercise leadership
Help clients and customers

Skills they need
Creative thinking
Responsibility
Speaking/listening

What Resort Workers Do

Resort workers assist the public at spas, luxury hotels, casinos, theme parks, and lodges. Resort employment opportunities range from entry-level housekeepers to ski instructors. The following section describes some of the types of jobs typically found in the industry.

Business departments employ *accountants*, *human resource specialists*, *managers*, *departmental supervisors*, and *general managers*, who handle administrative and organizational tasks.

Food service workers include *waiters*, who serve food to resort patrons in dining rooms and restaurants. *Bussers*, or *buspersons*, help set and clear tables and help the waitstaff serve food, especially when dealing with large parties. *Dishwashers* clean plates, glasses, utensils, and other cooking or serving implements. *Hosts* and *hostesses* show diners to their tables and may take dinner reservations over the phone. *Prep*

cooks, *sous chefs*, and *executive chefs* prepare all meals served at a resort.

Front desk workers include *desk clerks* and *reservation clerks*, who assign guests to their hotel room or guest quarters. They also give guests their mail or packages, take reservations over the phone, collect payment, and answer any questions regarding the resort. PBX operators work the resort switchboard, field calls, and sometimes take reservations.

Concierges assist resort guests with travel arrangements and reservations or provide information. The *bell staff*, supervised by the *bell captain*, bring guests' luggage to their rooms, run short errands, make deliveries, or drive resort vehicles. *Doormen* open doors for guests and help with the luggage.

The housekeeping and maintenance department employs *housekeepers* and *cleaners* to tidy guest rooms and common areas such as the lobby, dining rooms, and the pool and spa. *Maintenance workers* make

---

SCHOOL SUBJECTS
Mathematics, Speech

MINIMUM EDUCATION LEVEL
High school diploma

SALARY RANGE
$15,090 to $22,220 to $36,390 (plus tips)

OUTLOOK
About as fast as the average

OTHER ARTICLES TO READ
Cruise Ship Workers
Gaming Workers
Hotel and Motel Managers and Workers
Recreation Workers
Ski Resort Workers
Tour Guides

repairs throughout the resort ranging from mending broken chairs to fixing electrical circuits.

Security guards are employed to provide safety and security for all guests. Security personnel, especially if they are armed, must receive some sort of formal training.

Retail clerks and *retail managers* work at the shopping galleries and gift shops found at many resorts, selling everything from exclusive clothing and cosmetics to souvenirs to candy and snacks.

Specialty workers provide services advertised by the particular resort. *Lifeguards* supervise beaches and swimming pools. *Ski instructors* provide group or individual lessons for alpine resort patrons. Many beach resorts employ attendants to manage water activities such as water skiing, snorkeling, scuba diving, sailing, and deep-sea fishing. Dude ranches need *wranglers*, *trail guides*, and *horse grooms*. *Spa attendants* provide various facial, body, and water treatments.

Education and Training

A high school diploma is not required for resort work, though many resorts prefer high school graduates. If you are interested in something other than an entry-level position or wish to make this field a career, then a college education will be helpful.

Many companies look for graduates with backgrounds in hospitality, communications, or business management to fill higher-level management positions.

Outlook

Employment prospects in the resort industry will continue to be good. Large resorts in Las Vegas, the popularity of all-inclusive vacation packages, and alternative vacation destinations will supply endless employment opportunities for resort workers.

Management and hospitality graduates, entertainers, activity instructors, and chefs carry more responsibility and earn higher pay. Applicants with experience in the travel and tourism industry, or those who can speak a foreign language, will be in high demand.

For More Information

You may be able to find a job working at a nearby golf course, hotel, or restaurant. Pursue your interests in swimming, skiing, horseback riding, surfing, or sailing. Excelling in a particular activity is a good stepping-stone for a career in the resort industry.

National Ski Areas Association
133 South Van Gordon Street, Suite 300
Lakewood, CO 80228-1706
303-987-1111
nsaa@nsaa.org
http://www.nsaa.org

Resortjobs.com
180 State Road, Suite 2U
Sagamore Beach, MA 02562-2362
http://www.resortjobs.com

Travel Industry Association of America
1100 New York Avenue, NW, Suite 450
Washington, DC 20005-3934
202-408-8422
http://www.tia.org

Respiratory Therapists

SKILLS SPOTLIGHT
What they do
Help clients and customers
Select and apply tools/technology
Work with a team

Skills they need
Mathematics
Responsibility
Speaking/listening

What Respiratory Therapists Do

Respiratory therapists evaluate, treat, and care for patients with breathing disorders. These patients may be suffering from chronic conditions such as asthma or emphysema, or they may have been victims of heart failure, stroke, near drowning, or some other trauma. It is the respiratory therapist's job to try to restore the patient's full breathing capacity or monitor breathing with special equipment.

To evaluate which treatment is appropriate, respiratory therapists may first test lung capacity by having the patient breathe into a tube-shaped instrument that measures the amount and flow of air during inhalation and exhalation. They take these data and compare them to standardized data according to the patient's age, height, weight, and sex. Then therapists determine whether a lung deficiency exists. Another

test is the blood gas test, which analyzes the oxygen and carbon dioxide concentration in blood. The respiratory therapist draws an arterial blood sample, puts it in a special analyzer, and then reports the results to a physician.

After recommending a respiratory treatment, the therapist may administer oxygen to patients who cannot breathe on their own using a ventilator, which sends pressurized air into the lungs. Other treatments include having patients inhale medicine in aerosol form and performing chest physiotherapy, a procedure in which the therapist vibrates the patient's rib cage to loosen and drain mucus from the lungs.

Respiratory therapists see a variety of patients, such as premature infants whose lungs are not fully developed, elderly people with diseased lungs, or emergency-care patients who have suffered smoke inhalation or head injuries.

Monitoring and assessing patients' conditions is an important part of respiratory therapists' duties. They regularly check pa-

---

SCHOOL SUBJECTS
Health, Mathematics

MINIMUM EDUCATION LEVEL
Associate's degree

SALARY RANGE
$36,650 to $50,070 to $66,680

OUTLOOK
Faster than the average

OTHER ARTICLES TO READ
Diagnostic Medical Sonographers
Dialysis Technicians
Electroneurodiagnostic Technologists
Phlebotomy Technicians
Physical Therapy Assistants
X-ray Technologists

---

tients, and if a patient develops a problem, the therapist may recommend changes in treatment to physicians. Other duties include maintenance of equipment, keeping patient records up-to-date, tracking materials used, and recording patient charges.

Education and Training

High school graduates must get formal training to become respiratory therapists. Educational programs, which can be found at hospitals, medical schools, colleges, and trade schools, usually are two to four years in length. The Committee on Accreditation for Respiratory Care accredits some advanced-level programs that prepare you to be a Registered Respiratory Therapist (RRT). Entry-level programs prepare you to be a certified respiratory therapist (CRT). The CRT designation qualifies you for respiratory therapy technician positions.

Outlook

Employment growth for respiratory therapists is expected to be faster than the average through 2016, despite the fact that efforts to control rising health care costs have reduced the number of job opportunities in hospitals.

The increasing demand for therapists is the result of growth in neonatal care and gerontology services. Also, there is a greater incidence of cardiopulmonary and AIDS-related diseases, coupled with more advanced methods of diagnosing and treating them.

Employment opportunities should be available in home health care and hospi-

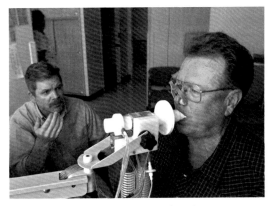

Respiratory therapists need to have mechanical ability and manual dexterity in order to be able to operate respiratory equipment. (Associated Press)

tal-based home health programs and with equipment rental companies and firms that provide respiratory care on a contract basis.

For More Information

Volunteer to work in a hospital, nursing home, or community health clinic to get experience working with patients and medical professionals.

American Association for Respiratory Care
9425 North MacArthur Boulevard, Suite 100
Irving, TX 75063-4706
972-243-2272
info@aarc.org
http://www.aarc.org

Committee on Accreditation for Respiratory Care
1248 Harwood Road
Bedford, TX 76021-4244
817-283-2835
http://www.coarc.com

Restaurant Managers

What Restaurant Managers Do

Restaurant managers are responsible for the overall operation of restaurants and other establishments that serve food. Managers usually hire and train their employees. *Food service manager*s are responsible for buying the food and equipment necessary for the operation of the restaurant or facility, and they may help with menu planning. They inspect the premises periodically to ensure compliance with health and sanitation regulations. Restaurant and food service managers perform many clerical and financial duties, such as keeping records, directing payroll operations, handling large sums of money, and taking inventories. Restaurant managers also usually supervise advertising and special sales programs.

The work of restaurant managers usually involves daily contact with customers. Managers take suggestions, handle complaints, and try to create a friendly atmosphere in which diners can enjoy themselves.

Very large restaurants may employ *assistant managers*, an *executive chef, food and beverage managers*, and a *wine steward* in addition to restaurant managers. These workers are trained to supervise the kitchen staff. They also are responsible for all food and drink preparation in the restaurant.

In some cases, the manager of a restaurant is also its owner. The owner-manager of a restaurant is likely to be involved in service functions, sometimes operating the cash register, waiting on tables, and performing a wide variety of tasks. Non-owner-managers of large restaurants or institutional food service facilities are usually employees who are paid a salary. They may work in dining rooms and cafeterias of hotels, department stores, factories, schools, hospitals, ships, trains, and private clubs.

Education and Training

Restaurant managers need to have experience in all areas of restaurant work before

SCHOOL SUBJECTS
Business, Health
MINIMUM EDUCATION LEVEL
High school diploma
SALARY RANGE
$28,240 to $44,570 to $74,060
OUTLOOK
About as fast as the average

OTHER ARTICLES TO READ
Bartenders
Business Managers
Caterers
Cooks, Chefs, and Bakers
Fast Food Workers
Food Production Workers
Food Service Workers

they can advance to the level of manager. They must be familiar with food preparation, food service, sanitary rules, and financial operations. Managers also must have good business skills in order to manage a budget and a staff. They apply this business knowledge as they buy machinery, equipment, and food.

Programs in restaurant management are offered by some colleges. These programs combine classroom work with on-the-job experience. Some graduates of technical or vocational schools can quickly qualify for management training.

Some managers learn their skills through a special apprenticeship program sponsored by the National Restaurant Association. Many restaurant managers start as waiters or kitchen staff, and as they gain on-the-job experience, they take on more responsibility and eventually move into management positions.

Outlook

Employment growth for well-qualified restaurant and food service managers will be as fast as the average through 2016, especially for those with bachelor's or associate's degrees. New restaurants are always opening to meet increasing demand.

❓ Did You Know?

The word *restaurant* comes from the French *restaurer*, meaning "to restore." The term was used in its present meaning for the first time in the 18th century.

Many job openings will arise from the need to replace managers retiring from the workforce. Also, population growth will result in an increased demand for eating establishments.

Economic downswings have a great effect on eating and drinking establishments. During a recession, people have less money to spend on luxuries such as dining out, thus hurting the restaurant business. However, greater numbers of working parents and their families are finding it convenient to eat out or purchase carryout food from a restaurant.

For More Information

You can learn about food preparation and food service by getting involved in planning and budgeting for family, church, or community events that involve food. Try to participate in every aspect of such events, including cooking, assigning tasks to others, buying ingredients and supplies, organizing dining areas, and hosting.

American Management Association
1601 Broadway
New York, NY 10019-7434
877-566-9441
customerservice@amanet.org
http://www.amanet.org

International Council on Hotel, Restaurant, and Institutional Education
2810 North Parham Road, Suite 230
Richmond, VA 23294-4422
804-346-4800
http://chrie.org

International Food Service Executives Association
500 Ryland Street, Suite 200
Reno, NV 89502-1676
800-893-5499
hq@ifsea.com
http://www.ifsea.org

Retail Business Owners

SKILLS SPOTLIGHT
What they do
Communicate ideas
Exercise leadership
Help clients and customers

Skills they need
Decision making
Mathematics
Speaking/listening

What Retail Business Owners Do

Retail business owners start or buy their own businesses or franchise operations. They are responsible for all aspects of a business operation, from planning and ordering merchandise to overseeing day-to-day operations. Retail business owners sell a wide variety of products, from apples to automobiles.

There are five general job categories in retail establishments: merchandising and buying, store operations, sales promotion and advertising, bookkeeping and accounting, and personnel supervision. *Merchandising and buying workers* determine the type and amount of goods to be sold. *Store operations workers* maintain the building and manage the movement of goods and personnel within the building. *Sales promotion and advertising workers* find ways to inform customers and potential customers about the goods and services that are available.

Bookkeeping and accounting workers keep records of payroll, taxes, and money spent and received. *Personnel workers* hire and train store staff.

Retail business owners must know about all five of these areas to make informed business decisions. Specific duties of an owner depend on the size of the store and the number of employees. In a store with more than 10 employees, many of the day-to-day operation, promotion, and personnel activities are supervised by managers, while the owner plans the overall purpose and function of the store. In a smaller store, the owner may handle most of the responsibilities, including sweeping the floor, greeting customers, balancing the accounting books, and placing ads in newspapers.

In both large and small operations, an owner has to keep up-to-date on product information as well as economic and technological conditions that may impact a business. Owners read catalogs about

SCHOOL SUBJECTS
Business, Mathematics

MINIMUM EDUCATION LEVEL
High school diploma

SALARY RANGE
$32,580 to $52,460 to $138,610

OUTLOOK
About as fast as the average

OTHER ARTICLES TO READ
Buyers
Cashiers
Counter and Retail Clerks
Merchandise Displayers
Purchasing Agents
Retail Sales Workers
Retail Store Managers
Sales Representatives

Fast Fact

The top five retailers (by annual sales) in the United States are Wal-Mart, Home Depot, Kroger, Costco, and Target.

products, check current inventories and prices, and research any technological advances that may make the operation more efficient.

Franchise owners obtain a license to sell an existing company's goods or services. The license agreement allows them to use expert advice from the sponsoring company about location, hiring and training of employees, arrangement of merchandise, advertising, and record keeping.

Education and Training

There are no specific educational or experience requirements for this position. Courses in mathematics, business management, accounting, typing, and computer science are helpful. Experience in the retail trade is recommended.

If you hope to own your own business someday, you are advised to earn a college degree. Appropriate areas of study include business communications, marketing, business law, business management, and accounting. You may want to earn a master's in business administration (M.B.A.) or in

another related graduate degree. There are also special business schools that offer one- or two-year programs in business management. Some correspondence schools also offer courses on how to plan and run a business.

Outlook

The retail field is extremely competitive, and many businesses fail each year. The most common reason for failure is poor management.

For More Information

Working part time as a sales clerk or stock clerk in a store is a good way to learn about the retail business. Read publications on self-employment, such as *Entrepreneur* magazine (https://www.entrepreneur.com).

Center for Women's Business Research
1760 Old Meadow Road, Suite 500
McLean, VA 22102-4306
703-556-7162
info@womensbusinessresearch.org
http://www.womensbusinessresearch.org

National Retail Federation
325 Seventh Street NW, Suite 1100
Washington, DC 20004-2825
800-673-4692
http://www.nrf.com

U.S. Small Business Administration
409 3rd Street, SW
Washington, DC 20416-0011
800-827-5722
answerdesk@sba.gov
http://www.sbaonline.sba.gov

Retail Sales Workers

What Retail Sales Workers Do

Retail sales workers assist customers in retail stores. They help customers decide what to buy, show them different products and how they work, take payment, record the sale, and arrange for delivery of the product, if necessary. Some other names for retail sales workers are *sales clerks*, *retail clerks*, *sales associates*, and *salespeople*.

A retail sales worker may have a wide range of duties. In a small retail store, the sales worker may take inventory, place newspaper ads, order goods, price merchandise, stock shelves, handle telephone calls, open the store in the morning, and lock it up at night. In a large department store, retail sales workers usually work in one department and have more limited duties.

Assisting customers is the priority for most retail sales workers. They help find the specific items customers want or suggest alternate choices. They may demon-strate products or give opinions on the quality of merchandise. When they are not waiting on customers, retail workers put price tags on items, stock shelves and racks, straighten and "face" product (place product so that labels are facing the customer), dust and clean products, and make sure aisles are clear.

With good skills, retail sales workers can move up to any of several positions. Some become the *senior salesperson* or head of their department. They manage the other employees in the department and may be responsible for placing orders for new merchandise. With experience, retail workers can also become *floor managers*, *branch managers*, and *general managers*. Some sales workers move on to become *buyers*, who decide what merchandise the store will carry and meet with manufacturers and designers to buy items for the store.

Some retail sales workers have a 40-hour workweek. In many stores, however, sales workers work 44 or 48 hours a week.

SCHOOL SUBJECTS
English, Mathematics, Speech

MINIMUM EDUCATION LEVEL
High school diploma

SALARY RANGE
$14,780 to $20,150 to $39,190

OUTLOOK
About as fast as the average

OTHER ARTICLES TO READ
Buyers
Cashiers
Clerks
Counter and Retail Clerks
Merchandise Displayers
Retail Store Managers
Sales Representatives

A retail sales worker shows a customer a piece of jewelry. (Rubberball Productions)

Working on evenings and weekends is often required, as is working long hours of overtime during the holiday seasons, when stores are the busiest. Workers in many stores have to stay past closing time to clean up the sales floor after a busy day.

Education and Training

Employers generally hire retail workers who are at least high school graduates, although there are some part-time opportunities available to high school students. Entry-level employees sometimes are asked to work in the store's stockroom at first so that they can learn more about the store's products and operations. They also may be asked to help set up displays or assist in the shipping department. After several months they may be promoted to sales workers.

Many employers prefer to hire college graduates, especially those with degrees in merchandising, business, or liberal arts. College graduates are more likely to be put directly into the store's management training program. Job applicants with pre-

vious retail sales experience also are considered good candidates for management training.

Outlook

The employment growth for sales personnel should be about as fast as the average for all occupations through 2016. Turnover among sales workers is much higher than average, creating a continual need to replace workers.

Several factors might reduce the long-range demand for sales personnel. As drug, variety, grocery, and other stores rapidly convert to self-service operations, they will need fewer sales workers. In contrast, many other stores are trying to stay competitive by offering better customer service and more sales staff attention.

There should continue to be good opportunities for temporary and part-time sales workers, especially during the holidays. Stores are particularly interested in people who, by returning year after year, develop good sales backgrounds and know the store's merchandise.

For More Information

Look for opportunities to develop your customer service skills. Volunteer to work at an information booth or sales booth at special events. Participate in fund-raising activities, such as bake sales, candy sales, and rummage sales.

National Retail Federation
325 Seventh Street, NW, Suite 1100
Washington, DC 20004-2825
800-673-4692
http://www.nrf.com

Retail Store Managers

What Retail Store Managers Do

Supermarkets, department stores, gift shops, and bakeries are just a few examples of retail stores. Store managers are in charge of everything that takes place in them, from hiring new employees to ensuring that the receipts add up at the end of the day. The store manager is often the first to arrive in the morning and the last to leave at night.

The most important skill for a good manager is knowing how to work with other people. Managers hire and train employees, assign their duties, and review salaries. There are bound to be disagreements and clashes from time to time, and managers must be able to keep arguments from getting out of control. Similarly, the store's customers may have complaints, and managers must be sensitive and understanding in dealing with the public.

Retail store managers track the merchandise in their stores. They keep accurate records so they know when to order new items, which items are the most popular, and which items are not selling.

Some managers handle all advertising and product promotions themselves, while others meet with advertising agency representatives and decide how best to advertise their store's merchandise. Managers often have the final say about which advertisements are sent to newspapers, radio, and television.

Other duties vary depending on the size of the store and the type of merchandise sold. In small stores, managers perform such duties as data processing, shipping, accounting, and sales. In large stores, managers may be responsible for a specific area, such as advertising or personnel.

Education and Training

Although some retail store managers do not have a college education, many large retail stores accept applications only from college graduates. If you are interested in this career, study English, advertising, ac-

---

SCHOOL SUBJECTS
Business, Mathematics

MINIMUM EDUCATION LEVEL
High school diploma

SALARY RANGE
$21,760 to $34,470 to $60,550

OUTLOOK
More slowly than the average

OTHER ARTICLES TO READ
Buyers
Cashiers
Merchandise Displayers
Retail Business Owners
Retail Sales Workers
Sales Representatives

---

counting, business, and marketing. All managers, regardless of their education, must have good marketing, analytical, and people skills.

Many large retail stores and national chains offer formal training programs, including classroom instruction, for their new employees. The training period may last a week or as long as a year. Training for a department store manager, for example, may include working as a salesperson in several departments to learn more about the store's business.

Part-time or summer jobs are good ways to enter this field. Often store managers are looking for salespeople because the turnover rate in these jobs is quite high. A salesperson who stays with a company and takes increasing responsibility is more likely to advance into a management position.

Outlook

Employment growth for retail managers is expected to be slower than the average for all occupations through the next decade. Although retailers have reduced their management staff to cut costs and make operations more efficient, there still are good opportunities in retailing. However, competition for jobs probably will continue to increase, and computerized systems for inventory control may reduce the need for some types of managers. Applicants with the best educational backgrounds and work experience will have the best chances of finding jobs.

One of a retail store manager's duties is to make sure that the inventory is properly stocked. (Getty Images)

For More Information

Volunteer to work at an information booth or sales booth at special events. Participate in fund-raising activities, such as bake sales, candy sales, and rummage sales. Read periodicals that publish articles on the retail industry, such as *Stores* online (http://www. stores.org), published by the National Retail Federation.

International Mass Retail Association
1700 North Moore Street, Suite 2250
Arlington, VA 22209-1933
703-841-2300
http://www.retail-leaders.org

National Retail Federation
325 Seventh Street, NW, Suite 1100
Washington, DC 20004-2825
800-673-4692
http://www.nrf.com

Retirement Planners

What Retirement Planners Do

Retirement planners are financial planners who specialize in the financial needs and concerns of people planning for retirement. Some retirement planners work for corporations of all sizes; many others are self-employed. Retirement planners have diverse backgrounds in fields such as banking, accounting, law, and life insurance.

To supplement the federal social security retirement income, people rely on pension plans, retirement accounts, and other forms of investments. Most workers today are aware of the importance of saving and planning for retirement, and they often turn to knowledgeable professionals for financial advice and strategies. The field of retirement planning grew as a specialty from traditional financial planning services. Such planners and counselors are in demand to create and administer financial retirement plans.

Retirement planners advise clients about important retirement issues such as relocation, medical insurance needs, income tax, wills, and estate planning. They also help prepare clients for the possibility of incapacity, disability, and the need for chronic-illness care during retirement. Disability income insurance, long-term care insurance, or a medical savings account may be suggested as precautions for such situations. Many companies, in an attempt to restructure or downsize, offer their employees the option for early retirement, complete with incentives. Retirement planners are consulted about the benefits or problems of early retirement.

Work as a retirement planner requires you to be in constant contact with your clients. You will need excellent communication skills and must be comfortable dealing with all kinds of people.

Education and Training

Take as many business and mathematics courses in high school as possible. Speech classes will help you develop oral communication skills, while English classes will

SCHOOL SUBJECTS
Business, Mathematics
MINIMUM EDUCATION LEVEL
Bachelor's degree
SALARY RANGE
$33,100 to $67,660 to $115,750
OUTLOOK
Faster than the average

OTHER ARTICLES TO READ
Accountants
Financial Analysts
Financial Planners
Financial Services Brokers

give you the basics necessary to write reports for your clients. Good computer skills are also a must.

A bachelor's degree is generally the basic requirement for a career in retirement planning. Most retirement planners and other financial advisers hold degrees in accounting, business, mathematics, or economics, as these directly relate to the type of work that planners do. Courses in taxes, estate planning, and risk management are especially helpful, and classes in communication and public speaking are important since interacting with clients is the cornerstone of this business.

Retirement planners may opt to become a chartered retirement plans specialist (CRPS) or a chartered retirement planning counselor (CRPC). CRPSs advise businesses on employee retirement plans, while CRPCs work with individuals who are retired or nearing retirement age. Certification requirements vary depending on the specialty, though all programs demand continuing education credits for yearly recertification.

Outlook

Employment opportunities for retirement planners are expected to increase faster than the average through 2016. The U.S. Census Bureau estimated that in 2000 there were 35 million people in the United States who were age 65 or older and that number is expected to increase to approximately 82 million people by the year 2050. The government's social security program often does not provide enough income to meet the financial needs of seniors as they continue to live longer and more productively. People are increasingly dependent on pension plans, savings plans, and investments to help maintain a comfortable standard of living through their retirement years. Financial planners, especially those who specialize in retirement plans, will be in high demand for their advice and recommendations on the best way to build and manage retirement funds.

For More Information

Check out the financial planning information available on the Internet to familiarize yourself with the industry.

Certified Financial Planner Board of Standards, Inc.
1425 K Street, NW, Suite 500
Washington, DC 20005-3686
800-487-1497
http://www.cfp-board.org

College for Financial Planning
8000 East Maplewood Avenue, Suite 800
Greenwood Village, CO 80111-4766
800-237-9990
http://www.cffp.edu

Financial Planning Association
4100 East Mississippi Avenue, Suite 400
Denver, CO 80246-3053
800-322-4237
http://www.fpanet.org

This retirement planner speaks with a couple about their future. (Getty Images)

Risk Managers

What they do
Communicate ideas
Exercise leadership
Help clients and customers

Skills they need
Mathematics
Reading/writing
Speaking/listening

What Risk Managers Do

Sometimes a business can fail or lose money over a problem that grows into a disaster because no one takes the proper steps to prevent it. *Risk managers* are the people responsible for trying to keep disasters from happening and for helping a business recover after a serious problem occurs. They monitor risks to a business and plan programs that reduce the chance of losses and damages.

Risk managers try to find all sources of potential problems in a company. Some examples of risk areas include fraud or criminal acts, injuries or death to an employee or someone outside of the company, property damage to a company, and loss of money because of the damage. A risk manager calculates how much money would be lost if any of these events were to happen.

Risk control is another important part of the job. After all potential problem areas have been identified, a risk manager decides the best ways to prevent damage from occurring. These may include providing safety training for employees, increasing security to protect against crime, or obtaining more insurance to cover lawsuits against the company. Because insurance costs have become more expensive, risk managers try to find ways in addition to purchasing insurance by which a company can protect itself.

Risk managers must be well informed about all aspects of a business to predict problem areas. They regularly inspect machinery and equipment for safety and ensure that employees have a safe place to work. They also make sure employees follow safety procedures, such as wearing hardhats or protective clothing.

Many risk managers are employed in oil, drug, or communications companies. However, all types of industries need people to evaluate and prevent risks. In large firms, a risk manager may be a vice president with many people on his or her staff. Some companies have risk management departments, and the managers have assigned areas. For

SCHOOL SUBJECTS
Business, Mathematics

MINIMUM EDUCATION LEVEL
Bachelor's degree

SALARY RANGE
$42,280 to $70,400 to $137,210

OUTLOOK
About as fast as the average

OTHER ARTICLES TO READ
Accountants
Cost Estimators
Credit Analysts
Financial Analysts
Insurance Underwriters
Management Analysts and Consultants

Fast Fact

The field of risk management has existed only since the 1950s. The growth of technology led to the expansion of the field as companies sought to prevent, minimize, and finance losses associated with implementing new technology and new business models.

instance, one manager may deal with fraud and property damage. Another might be in charge of employee injuries or insurance. In smaller companies, managers also may be in charge of safety training, employee benefits, and other personnel tasks.

Education and Training

If risk management interests you, you should plan to earn a bachelor's degree in business management, finance, or accounting. Classes in mathematics, economics, and accounting will be useful. Computer skills also are an advantage. You need to have a broad knowledge of many fields, including chemistry, law, engineering, and insurance. Some people who plan to become risk managers prefer to obtain a degree in one of these specialized subjects.

Many organizations require their risk managers to earn the designation Associate in Risk Management (ARM) or Certified Risk Manager (CRM). The ARM program is run jointly by the American Institute for Chartered Property Casualty Underwriters and the Insurance Institute of America.

The Certified Risk Managers International, a member of the National Alliance for Insurance Education & Research, offers the CRM program.

Outlook

The need for risk management is expected to grow about as fast as the average through 2016. Organizations now recognize risk management as an important and effective tool to manage costs. The profession will continue to gain recognition in the next decade, so salaries and career opportunities are expected to continue to increase.

For More Information

Look for opportunities to participate in financial activities. Volunteer to be the treasurer for school clubs or community organizations you belong to. Read books about general business practices, the history of insurance, and the different kinds of insurance available today.

American Risk and Insurance Association
716 Providence Road
Malvern, PA 19355-0728
610-640-1997
aria@cpcuiia.org
http://www.aria.org

National Alliance for Insurance Education & Research
PO Box 27027
Austin, TX 78755-2027
800-633-2165
alliance@scic.com
http://www.scic.com

Risk and Insurance Management Society, Inc.
1065 Avenue of the Americas, 13th Floor
New York, NY 10018-1878
212-286-9292
http://www.rims.org

Road Crew Workers

What Road Crew Workers Do

The heavy traffic of cars and trucks does a lot of damage to streets and highways. Harsh weather also causes damage, resulting in potholes and broken pavement. *Road crew workers* help maintain and repair the roadways, which include country roads, freeways, bike paths, and runways. They build new roads, repave old roads, clear snow and ice, and cut the grass at the sides of highways. Other tasks might include putting up signs, directing traffic, operating trucks and tractors, and preparing asphalt and concrete for spreading across the road's surface.

Supervising road crew workers look at blueprints, drawings, and surveys to determine what materials, tools, and workers will be required to complete the project. They help determine how much time will be needed for the project and if traffic will have to be redirected onto other roadways. Other workers set up barricades and lights to warn drivers of construction, direct drivers into alternate lanes, and post lower speed limits. Those who direct traffic may be required to stand in the street with signs and to communicate with the other road workers using walkie-talkies. Road crew workers always wear reflective vests and follow other safety procedures.

In road construction or repair projects, the first step is to clear land or remove old pavement. Road crew workers level the ground and spread out crushed stone and gravel. The crew may install steel and wire to strengthen the base of the roadway. Road crew workers drive the trucks and operate the tractors for these operations. Once the concrete or asphalt is prepared, they pour and spread the material from a cement mixer or spreader. With special finishing tools, they shape the curbs and drains. They then prepare the surface by rubbing it with stones and sealing it with chemicals.

During winter months, road crew workers operate snowplows and salt trucks. During warm weather, they clean brush from

SCHOOL SUBJECTS	
Mathematics, Technical/Shop	
MINIMUM EDUCATION LEVEL	
High school diploma	
SALARY RANGE	
$17,410 to $27,310 to $51,750	
OUTLOOK	
About as fast as the average	

OTHER ARTICLES TO READ
Construction Laborers
Industrial Machinery Mechanics
Operating Engineers
Stationary Engineers
Truck Drivers

roadsides, mow grass, and clean up litter. Road crew workers work outdoors in all kinds of weather.

Education and Training

You may need a high school diploma for some road maintenance work, but it is not always required. Experience with a construction crew, a summer road crew, or farm work can help you learn about operating and repairing heavy machinery and trucks. You will definitely need a high school diploma and further training if you hope to advance to better-paying positions. Most community colleges offer courses in mechanics and heavy equipment.

Outlook

Employment growth for all operating engineers is projected to be about as fast as the average through 2016. Many road crew workers are employed by local governments. These workers handle the construction and repair of highways, bridges, dams, harbors, airports, subways, water and sewage systems, power plants, and transmission lines. Construction of schools, offices and other commercial buildings, and residential properties will also stimulate demand for these workers. However, the construction industry is very sensitive to changes in the overall economy, so the number of openings may fluctuate from year to year.

For More Information

Visit the Web sites of your state's department of transportation for information about road projects. For links go to http://www.tdot.state.tn.us/links.htm. The U.S. Department of Transportation Web site,

These road crew workers are working alongside an asphalt paving machine, smoothing a new stretch of road. (Dwight Smith/Shutterstock)

http://www.dot.gov, also offers information and links to other related agencies.

Associated General Contractors of America
2300 Wilson Boulevard, Suite 400
Arlington, VA 22201-5426
703-548-3118
info@agc.org
http://www.agc.org

International Union of Operating Engineers
1125 17th Street, NW
Washington, DC 20036-4701
202-429-9100
http://www.iuoe.org

Robotics Engineers and Technicians

SKILLS SPOTLIGHT

What they do
Create or improve systems
Help clients and customers
Select and apply tools/technology

Skills they need
Mathematics
Problem solving
Speaking/listening

What Robotics Engineers and Technicians Do

Robotics engineers use computer technology to design, develop, build, and program robotic devices. They understand manufacturing production requirements and how robots can best be used in automated systems to achieve cost efficiency, productivity, and quality. Robotics engineers analyze and evaluate a manufacturer's operating system to determine whether robots can be used efficiently instead of humans and other automated equipment.

Robotics technicians help engineers make and operate robots. Robots are machines that perform tasks ordinarily done by humans. Computers control the movement and actions of robots. Many industries use robots to do very precise or complicated tasks that are often repetitive. Robots can assemble delicate computer parts or tend the machines that weave cloth. Many industrial robots do not look like human beings; for example, an industrial robot may simply be a mechanical arm.

Robotics technicians assist with every phase of making robots. After robotics engineers design a robot, the technicians conduct tests to make sure the design will work. Then they help build a model. If the model works, the technicians help draw up the blueprints that show how to manufacture the design.

Some robotics technicians work on assembling robots. They may obtain the needed materials and parts, or they may put together and install special mechanical or electrical parts of a robot. They may also work on testing the finished robots to make sure they perform correctly.

Other robotics technicians operate robots or teach other employees how to use and maintain robots. Some technicians

SCHOOL SUBJECTS
Computer science, Mathematics
MINIMUM EDUCATION LEVEL
Bachelor's degree (robotics engineers) High school diploma (robotics technicians)
SALARY RANGE
$46,340 to $71,430 to $104,490 (robotics engineers) $31,130 to $47,490 to $79,020 (robotics technicians)
OUTLOOK
About as fast as the average

OTHER ARTICLES TO READ
Electrical and Electronics Engineers
Electronics Engineering Technicians
Hardware Engineers
Industrial Engineers and Engineering
 Technicians

travel to different factories to maintain and repair their robots.

Robotics technicians who work on design and testing usually work in comfortable offices; those who assemble, operate, or maintain robots may work in noisy factories.

Education and Training

To prepare for a career in robotics, take as many science, mathematics, and computer classes as possible. Other useful classes are blueprint reading, electronics, and machine shop.

A high school diploma is required for a career as a robotics technician. Most employers prefer to hire people who have completed a two-year program in robotics, industrial technology, or manufacturing engineering.

To become an engineer you must earn a bachelor of science degree. Some colleges and universities offer robotics engineering degrees, and others offer engineering degrees with concentrations or options in robotics and manufacturing engineering. For some higher-level jobs, such as robotics designer, a master of science or doctoral degree is required.

Outlook

Employment opportunities for robotics engineers and technicians are closely tied to economic conditions in the United States and in the global marketplace. The United States is the world's second-largest robotics user next to Japan.

For More Information

Participate in school science clubs and fairs and pursue hobbies that involve electronics, mechanical equipment, and model building. Complete robot kits are available through a number of companies and range from simple, inexpensive robots to highly complex robots with advanced features and accessories.

Association for Unmanned Vehicle Systems International
2700 South Quincy Street, Suite 400
Arlington, VA 22206-2226
703-845-9671
info@auvsi.org
http://www.auvsi.org

Robotic Industries Association
900 Victors Way, Suite 140
PO Box 3724
Ann Arbor, MI 48106-3724
734-994-6088
http://www.roboticsonline.com

Robotics and Automation Society
Institute of Electrical and Electronics Engineers
1828 L Street, NW, Suite 1202
Washington, DC 20036-5104
202-530-8347
http://www.ncsu.edu/IEEE-RAS

Robotics engineer Tobias Kaupp prepares to launch a robotic submarine into the water surrounding Australia's Great Barrier Reef. These robotic submarines are used to collect data and perform underwater research. (AFP/Getty Images)

Roman Catholic Priests

What Roman Catholic Priests Do

Roman Catholic priests serve as either *diocesan priests* (sometimes called *secular priests*) who lead individual parishes within a certain diocese, or as *religious priests* who live and work with other members of their religious order. In the Roman Catholic Church, only men are called to the priesthood. A vow of celibacy is required, along with vows of poverty and obedience. The primary function of all priests is administering the church's seven sacraments: baptism, confirmation, confession, Holy Communion, marriage, holy orders, and last rites.

Diocesan priests generally work in parishes and are responsible for leading liturgical celebrations, especially the mass. They also provide pastoral care for their parishioners in times of sickness, death, or personal crisis. Diocesan priests oversee the religious education of everyone in their congregation and take care of administrative duties. Some work in parochial schools attached to parish churches or in diocesan high schools.

Religious priests, such as Dominicans, Jesuits, or Franciscans, work as members of a religious community, teaching, doing missionary work, or engaging in other specialized activities as assigned by their superiors.

Priests may serve in a wide range of ministries, from counseling full time and working in social services to being chaplains in the armed forces, prisons, or hospitals. Like all clergy, priests prepare sermons and follow current religious and secular events.

In addition to having a strong desire to help others, priests need to be able to communicate effectively and supervise others. They must have common sense, initiative, and self-confidence to oversee a parish or mission. They also must have compassion, humility, and integrity to set an example for others.

SCHOOL SUBJECTS	
English, Religion	
MINIMUM EDUCATION LEVEL	
Bachelor's degree	
SALARY RANGE	
$20,240 to $40,460 to $70,670	
OUTLOOK	
Faster than the average	
OTHER ARTICLES TO READ	
Grief Therapists	
Guidance Counselors	
Protestant Ministers	
Rabbis	
Religious Sisters and Brothers	
Social Workers	

Roman Catholic priests perform regular masses as well as services for weddings, christenings, and funerals. (Richard Welter/Shutterstock)

Education and Training

In preparing for the priesthood, you should be conscientious about living the Catholic faith as fully as you can. Attend mass and other services frequently, read about church history and doctrine, and take part in parish activities. You need a strong religious faith and the belief that you have received a special call from God to serve and help others.

Some Catholic high schools offer preparation for the priesthood similar to that of a college preparatory high school. High school seminary studies focus on English, speech, literature, and social studies. Latin may or may not be required; the study of other foreign languages, especially Spanish, is encouraged.

Eight years of postsecondary study usually are required to become an ordained priest. The last four years of preparation for ordination are devoted to the study of theology, including studies in ethics and doctrine. In the third year of advanced training, candidates undertake fieldwork in parishes and the wider community.

Outlook

There is a shortage of priests in the Roman Catholic Church. In the last 30 years, the number of priests has declined by about 25 percent because of retirement and those leaving the profession for other reasons. Opportunities for positions in the priesthood are increasing and will probably continue to do so for the foreseeable future. Priests are needed in all areas of the country, but the greatest need is in metropolitan areas that have large Catholic populations and in communities near Catholic educational institutions.

As a result of the continuing shortage of priests, the number of ordained deacons has increased. Deacons are not authorized to celebrate mass or administer the sacraments of reconciliation and the anointing of the sick. They can preach and perform baptisms, marriages, and funerals; and provide service to the community.

For More Information

Talk with your parish priest and others involved in the pastoral work of the church to get a clearer idea of the responsibilities of priesthood. Your priest or diocesan vocations office can put you in touch with a religious order if that is where you would like to serve.

National Federation of Priests' Councils
333 North Michigan Avenue, Suite 1205
Chicago, IL 60601-4002
888-271-6372
nfpc@nfpc.org
http://www.nfpc.org

National Religious Vocation Conference
5401 Cornell Avenue, Suite 207
Chicago, IL 60615-5604
773-363-5454
http://www.nrvc.net

Roofers

What Roofers Do

Roofers apply roofing materials, including tile and slate shingles, to the roofs of buildings. They also waterproof and damp-proof walls, swimming pools, and other building surfaces. Although roofers usually are trained to apply most kinds of roofing, they often specialize in either sheet membrane roofing or prepared roofings such as asphalt shingles, slate, or tile.

The most common type of roofing is composition roofing. In one type of composition roofing, called built-up roofing, roofers place overlapping strips of asphalt or tar-coated felt to the roof. Then they spread a thin layer of hot asphalt or coal tar pitch over the felt strips. The roofers continue alternating felt strips and hot asphalt or pitch until they reach the desired thickness. Finally, a topcoat of coal tar pitch and gravel or a smooth coat of asphalt is applied. On some composition roofs, asphalt shingles or rolls of roofing material are affixed with nails or asphalt cement.

Another type of composition roofing is single-ply roofing. Single-ply roofs differ from built-up roofs in the way their seams are sealed: contact adhesive cements, hot-air welders, solvent welding, and propane or butane torches are used. Many manufacturers of these systems require that roofers take special courses and receive certification before they are allowed to use the products.

Tile and slate shingles, which are more expensive types of residential roofing, are installed a little differently. First, roofing felt is applied over the wood base. Next, the roofers punch holes in the slate or tile pieces so that nails can be inserted, or they embed the tiles in mortar. Each row of shingles overlaps the preceding row.

Metal roofing is applied by roofers or by sheet metal workers. One type of metal roof uses metal sections shaped like flat pans, soldered together for weatherproofing and attached by metal clips to the wood below. Standing seam roofing has

SCHOOL SUBJECTS
Mathematics, Technical/Shop

MINIMUM EDUCATION LEVEL
Apprenticeship

SALARY RANGE
$21,290 to $33,240 to $56,680

OUTLOOK
About as fast as the average

OTHER ARTICLES TO READ
Carpenters
Construction Laborers
Drywall Installers and Finishers
Floor Covering Installers
Road Crew Workers
Sheet Metal Workers

raised seams where the sections of sheet metal interlock.

Roofers may waterproof and damp-proof structures other than roofs. First, the roofers smooth rough surfaces and slightly roughen glazed surfaces. Then they apply waterproofing fabric to the surface, either with a brush or by spraying. Damp-proofing, which prevents moisture from penetrating building surfaces, is done by spraying a coat of tar or asphalt onto the building surfaces.

Roofers work outdoors most of the time. They work in the heat and cold, but not in wet weather. The work is physically strenuous, involving lifting heavy weights, standing, climbing, bending, and squatting. Roofers must work while standing on surfaces that may be steep and quite high.

Education and Training

Employers prefer to hire applicants who are at least 18 years old and who have earned a high school diploma. Roofers must complete an apprenticeship or on-the-job training program. Apprenticeships usually last three years, and on-the-job training lasts four or five years. All roofers should receive safety training that is in compliance with Occupational Safety and Health Administration (OSHA) standards. Workers can get safety training through their employer or through OSHA's Outreach Training Program.

Outlook

Employment for roofers is expected to increase about as fast as the average for all occupations through 2016. Roofers will continue to be in demand for the construction of new buildings, and roofs tend to need more maintenance and repair work.

Roofers learn to layer tiles on roofs in ways that keep the inside of the house warm and dry. (Shutterstock)

For More Information

Check your library or bookstore for books about roofing techniques, such as *The Roofing Handbook* by Robert Scharff and Terry Kennedy (McGraw-Hill Professional Publishing, 2000) or *Structure, Roofing, and the Exterior* by Alan Carson and Robert Dunlop (Stoddart Publishing, 2000). Watch how-to videos on roofing and other construction specialties.

National Roofing Contractors Association
10255 West Higgins Road, Suite 600
Rosemont, IL 60018-5607
847-299-9070
http://www.nrca.net

United Union of Roofers, Waterproofers and Allied Workers
1660 L Street, NW, Suite 800
Washington, DC 20036-5646
202-463-7663
roofers@unionroofers.com
http://www.unionroofers.com

Roustabouts

What Roustabouts Do

Roustabouts do most of the routine physical work in the oil and gas industry. They help around the wells that produce oil and natural gas, and they work on the pipelines and barges that transport oil and gas.

Roustabouts' work varies from place to place and from job to job. They may clear sites that have been selected for drilling and build a solid base for drilling equipment. They cut down trees to make way for roads or to reduce fire hazards. They dig trenches for foundations, fill excavated areas, mix up batches of wet concrete, and pour concrete into building forms. Other jobs include loading and unloading pipe and other materials onto or from trucks and boats.

Roustabouts also dig drainage ditches around wells, storage tanks, and other installations. They walk flow lines to locate leaks and clean up spilled oil by bailing it into barrels or other containers. They also clean and repair oil field machinery and equipment.

Other duties that roustabouts perform include driving and unloading trucks; painting equipment such as storage tanks and pumping units; assembling, operating, and repairing machinery such as boilers, pumps, and valves; and cleaning up work sites. Basically, roustabouts do whatever routine physical work and maintenance their supervisor tells them to do.

The tools roustabouts use range from simple hand tools like hammers and shovels to heavy equipment such as backhoes or trackhoes. Roustabouts use heavy wrenches and other hand tools to help break out and replace pipe, valves, and other components for repairs or modifications and truck winches for moving or lifting heavy items. Roustabouts also operate motorized lifts, power tools, and electronic sensors and testers. They also may operate tractors with shredders, forklifts, or ditching machines.

Roustabouts who work for drilling contractors usually travel from place to place as

SCHOOL SUBJECTS
Mathematics, Technical/Shop

MINIMUM EDUCATION LEVEL
Apprenticeship

SALARY RANGE
$19,090 to $28,510 to $46,220

OUTLOOK
More slowly than the average

OTHER ARTICLES TO READ
Coal Mining Technicians
Construction Laborers
Operating Engineers
Petroleum Engineers and Technicians
Petroleum Refining Workers
Road Crew Workers
Stevedores

These roustabouts are working on an oil rig in Kern County, California. (Richard Thornton/Shutterstock)

they work on one job after another. Roustabouts who work on producing wells usually stay at one location for longer periods of time. Those who work on offshore wells may live on the rig for one to four weeks at a time before coming to shore for an equal amount of time off.

Education and Training

Although there are no formal requirements for roustabouts, firms prefer to hire high school graduates. Applicants with mechanical skills and those who have taken technical courses have an edge in the job market. Classes in mathematics and technical training are helpful.

Most roustabouts receive informal on-the-job training about safety, equipment and machine maintenance, and oil and gas field operations. More and more applicants are graduates of an associate's degree program in petroleum technology.

Outlook

The number of roustabout jobs is expected to grow slower than the average through 2016 due to continuing advances in oil field automation, changes in production methods, and recent difficulties in the oil and gas industries.

Despite the problems in the industry, oil and gas will continue to be primary energy sources. While few new jobs for roustabouts are expected to develop, they always will be needed, and there will be some openings as turnover is high among roustabouts, especially in offshore drilling. Workers who have experience or formal training in the field will have the best chance of being hired.

For More Information

You can find links to energy-related Web sites at http://www.industrylink.com. If you live near an oil field, you may be able to arrange a tour by contacting the public relations departments of oil companies or drilling contractors.

American Petroleum Institute
1220 L Street, NW
Washington, DC 20005-4070
202-682-8000
http://www.api.org

Society of Petroleum Engineers
PO Box 833836
Richardson, TX 75083-3836
800-456-6863
spedal@spe.org
http://www.spe.org

University of Texas at Austin
Petroleum Extension Service
1 University Station, R8100
Austin, TX 78712-1100
800-687-4132
http://www.utexas.edu/cee/petex

Sales Representatives

What Sales Representatives Do

Sales representatives sell goods to retail stores, other manufacturers and wholesalers, government agencies, and various institutions. They usually cover a specific geographic area. Some representatives concentrate on just a few products. An electrical appliance salesperson, for example, may sell 10 to 30 items ranging from food freezers and air conditioners to waffle irons and portable heaters. Representatives of drug wholesalers, however, may sell as many as 50,000 different items.

Sales representatives locate and contact potential clients, keep up a regular correspondence with existing customers, determine their clients' needs, and inform clients about products and prices. They travel to meet with clients, show them samples or catalogs, take orders, arrange for delivery, and sometimes provide installation. Sales representatives also handle customer complaints, keep up-to-date on new products, and prepare reports. Many salespeople attend trade conferences, where they learn about products and make sales contacts.

The particular products sold by the sales representative directly affect the nature of the work. Salespeople who represent sporting goods manufacturers may spend most of their time driving from town to town calling on retail stores that carry sporting equipment. They may visit with coaches and athletic directors of high schools and colleges. A representative in this line may be a former athlete or coach who knows intimately the concerns of his or her customers.

Food manufacturers and wholesalers employ large numbers of sales representatives, who negotiate with retail merchants to obtain the most advantageous store and shelf position for displaying their products.

Direct, or door-to-door, selling has been an effective way of marketing various products, such as appliances and housewares, cookware, china, tableware and linens,

SCHOOL SUBJECTS
Business, Mathematics

MINIMUM EDUCATION LEVEL
High school diploma

SALARY RANGE
$26,490 to $50,750 to $103,910

OUTLOOK
About as fast as the average

OTHER ARTICLES TO READ
Buyers
Merchandise Displayers
Purchasing Agents
Retail Sales Workers
Retail Store Managers
Services Sales Representatives

Fast Fact

In the United States, about two million people work as manufacturers' and wholesale sales representatives.

foods, drugs, cosmetics and toiletries, costume jewelry, clothing, and greeting cards. Like other sales representatives, door-to-door sales workers find prospective buyers, explain and demonstrate their products, and take orders. Door-to-door selling has waned in popularity, and Internet selling has taken over much of the door-to-door market.

Education and Training

A high school diploma is required for most sales positions, and an increasing number of salespeople are graduates of two- or four-year colleges. The more complex a product, the greater the likelihood that it will be sold by a college-trained person.

Some areas of sales work require specialized college work. Those in engineering sales, for example, usually have a college degree in an engineering field. Other fields that require salespeople to have specific college degrees include chemical sales, office systems, and pharmaceuticals and drugs.

Outlook

Employment growth for sales representatives is expected to be about as fast as the average through 2016 due to continued increases in the variety and amount of products sold. Future opportunities will vary greatly depending upon the specific product and industry. For example, as giant food chains replace independent grocers, fewer salespeople will be needed to sell groceries to individual stores. By contrast, greater opportunities will probably exist in the air-conditioning field, and advances in consumer electronics and computer technology also may provide many new opportunities.

For More Information

Junior Achievement (http://www.ja.org) programs can introduce you to economic concepts, including buying and selling goods and services.

Direct Marketing Association
Educational Foundation
1120 Avenue of the Americas
New York, NY 10036-6700
212-768-7277
http://www.the-dma.org

Manufacturers' Agents National Association
16 A Journey, Suite 200
Aliso Viejo, CA 92656-3317
877-626-2776
MANA@MANAonline.org
http://www.manaonline.org

School Administrators

SKILLS SPOTLIGHT

What they do
Communicate ideas
Exercise leadership
Work with a team

Skills they need
Decision making
Reading/writing
Speaking/listening

What School Administrators Do

School administrators oversee the operation of schools or entire school districts. They work with either public or private schools. Those who work as administrators in private schools are often called *headmasters*, *headmistresses*, or *school directors*. They make sure students, teachers, and other employees follow educational guidelines and meet budget requirements.

There are two basic kinds of school administrators in public schools: *principals* and *superintendents*. School principals hire and assign teachers and other staff, help them improve their skills, make sure they are using approved teaching methods, and evaluate their performance. Principals plan and evaluate the instructional programs jointly with teachers. They visit classrooms and examine learning materials. They also supervise the school's counselors and other staff members. They review the students'

performance and decide how to handle students with learning or behavior problems. Principals resolve conflicts that students and teachers may have with one another, with parents, or with school board policies. In larger schools, they may be aided by *assistant principals*, sometimes called *deans of students*.

School superintendents manage the affairs of an entire school district, which may range in size from a small town with a handful of schools to a city with a population of millions. Superintendents are elected by the board of education to oversee and coordinate the activities of all the schools in the district in accordance with board of education standards. They select and employ staff and negotiate contracts. They manage budgets, the acquisition and maintenance of school buildings, and the purchase and distribution of school supplies and equipment.

Superintendents coordinate activities with other school districts and agencies. They speak before community and civic groups and try to enlist their support. In

SCHOOL SUBJECTS
Business, English
MINIMUM EDUCATION LEVEL
Master's degree
SALARY RANGE
$37,800 to $69,300 to $119,250
OUTLOOK
Faster than the average

OTHER ARTICLES TO READ
College Administrators
College Professors
Elementary School Teachers
Guidance Counselors
Secondary School Teachers
Special Education Teachers

📊 Growth Field

Between 2006 and 2016 the number of administrators in preschool and young child education is expected to grow from 56,000 to 69,000, an increase of about 24 percent.

addition, they collect statistics, prepare reports, enforce compulsory attendance, and oversee the operation of the school transportation system and the provision of health services.

Education and Training

Most principals and assistant principals have had years of teaching experience and hold master's degrees in educational administration. Most states require school principals to be licensed, but licensing requirements vary from state to state. Private schools are not subject to state certification requirements, so some private school principals and assistant principals may hold only a bachelor's degree. Most, however, have master's degrees. A doctorate in educational administration is often required for school superintendents.

Outlook

Employment opportunities for school administrators are expected to increase faster than the average through 2016. There is a shortage of qualified candidates to fill superintendent positions in public schools, and the number of school-age children is expected to increase over the next decade adding to the need for administrators. Job prospects will be good for principals as well.

For More Information

Talk to your teachers about their work, and offer to assist them with some projects before or after school. You can gain experience in the education field by teaching Sunday school classes, getting a summer job as a camp counselor or day care center aide, working with a scouting group, volunteering to coach a youth athletic team, or tutoring younger students.

American Association of School Administrators
801 North Quincy Street, Suite 700
Arlington, VA 22203-1730
703-528-0700
info@aasa.org
http://www.aasa.org

National Association of Elementary School Principals
1615 Duke Street
Alexandria, VA 22314-3406
703-684-3345
naesp@naesp.org
http://www.naesp.org

National Association of Secondary School Principals
1904 Association Drive
Reston, VA 20191-1537
703-860-0200
http://www.nassp.org

Science and Medical Writers

What Science and Medical Writers Do

Science and medical writers translate technical medical and scientific information so it can be published and distributed to the general public and professionals in the field. They write for books, magazines, newsletters, brochures, academic journals, radio and television broadcasts, and the Internet.

Science and medical writers research a topic to gain a thorough understanding of the subject matter. This may require hours of research on the Internet or in libraries. Writers may also interview professionals such as doctors, pharmacists, scientists, engineers, managers, and other experts on the subject. They sometimes obtain graphs, photos, illustrations, or historical facts to help explain the story.

In addition to knowing the subject matter, writers must know the audience they are writing for and how to reach it. For example, if reporting on a new heart surgery procedure that will soon be available to the public, writers may need to explain why and how the surgery is performed. They may give a basic overview and illustration of how a healthy heart works, show a diseased heart in comparison, and report on how this surgery can help the patient. The public will also want to know how many people are affected by this disease, what the symptoms are, how many procedures have been done successfully, where they were performed, what the recovery time is, and if there are any complications. In addition, interviews with doctors and patients add a personal touch to the story.

Some science and medical writers specialize in a particular subject. For instance, a medical writer may write only about cardiology. Science writers may limit their writing or research to environmental science, or they may be even more specific and focus only on air pollution issues.

Some writers choose to be freelance writers either on a full-time or part-time basis. Freelance science and medical writers are self-employed writers.

Education and Training

There are two avenues to becoming a science and medical writer. You may begin by earning an undergraduate degree in English, journalism, or liberal arts and then obtain a master's degree in a communications field, such as medical or science writing. The second path is to earn a degree in one of the sciences or a medicine-related field and then develop your writing skills. In either case, a good liberal arts education is important, since you are often required to write about many subject areas. You may be able to find internship programs in the communications department of a corporation, medical institution, or research facility.

Outlook

There is a lot of competition for writing and editing jobs. However, the demand for writers and editors is expected to grow about as fast as the average through 2016 due to the growing numbers of print and online publications. As more advances occur in medicine, science, and technology, there will continue to be a demand for skilled writers to relay that information to the public and other professionals.

For More Information

Work as a reporter or writer on school newspapers, yearbooks, and literary magazines. Attend writing workshops and take writing classes to practice and sharpen your skills. Part-time or volunteer work at health care facilities, newspapers, publishing companies, or scientific research facilities can also provide experience and insight regarding this career. Read science and medical articles in major newspapers such as the *New York Times* or the *Wall Street Journal*.

American Medical Writers Association
30 West Gude Drive, Suite 525
Rockville, MD 20850-1162
301-294-5303
amwa@amwa.org
http://www.amwa.org

National Association of Science Writers Inc.
PO Box 7905
Berkeley, CA 94707-0905
510-647-9500
http://www.nasw.org

Society for Technical Communication
901 North Stuart Street, Suite 904
Arlington, VA 22203-1821
703-522-4114
stc@stc.org
http://www.stc.org

 Did You Know?

Gray's Anatomy, an illustrated anatomy textbook was originally published in 1858. This book is still in print and as of 2008 was in its 40th edition.

Screenwriters

What Screenwriters Do

Screenwriters write scripts for motion pictures or television. The themes may be their own ideas or stories assigned by a producer or director. Often, screenwriters are hired to turn popular plays or novels into screenplays. Writers of original screenplays create their own stories that are produced for the motion picture industry or television. Screenwriters may also write television programs, such as comedies, dramas, documentaries, variety shows, and entertainment specials.

Screenwriters must not only be creative, but they must also have excellent research skills. For projects such as historical movies, documentaries, and medical or science programs, research is a very important step. A screenwriter also must have a creative imagination and the ability to tell a story.

Screenwriters start with an outline, or a treatment of the story's plot. When the director or producer approves the story outline, screenwriters then complete the story

for production. During the writing process, screenwriters write many drafts of the script. They frequently meet with directors and producers to discuss script changes.

Some screenwriters work alone, and others work on teams with other writers. Many specialize in certain types of scripts, such as dramas, comedies, documentaries, motion pictures, or television. *Motion picture screenwriters* usually write alone and exclusively for movies. Screenwriters for television series work very long hours in the studio. Many television shows have limited runs, so much of the work for *television screenwriters* is not continuous.

Scripts are written in a two-column format, one column for dialogue and sound, the other for video instructions. One page of script equals about one minute of running time, though it varies. Each page has about 150 words and takes about 20 seconds to read. Screenwriters send a query letter outlining their idea before they submit a script to a production company. Then they send a standard release form and wait at least a month for a response. Studios buy

---

SCHOOL SUBJECTS
English, Theater/Dance

MINIMUM EDUCATION LEVEL
High school diploma

SALARY RANGE
$26,530 to $50,660 to $99,910

OUTLOOK
About as fast as the average

OTHER ARTICLES TO READ
Actors
Cinematographers
Film and Television Directors
Literary Agents
Writers

many more scripts than are actually produced, and studios often will buy a script only with provisions that the original writer or another writer will rewrite it to their specifications.

Education and Training

In high school, you should develop your writing skills in English, theater, speech, and journalism classes. Social studies and foreign language can also be helpful in creating intelligent scripts.

The best way to prepare for a career as a screenwriter is to write and read every day. A college degree is not required, but a liberal arts education is helpful because it exposes you to a wide range of subjects. Schools with film programs usually have screenwriting courses. While in school, become involved in theater to learn about all of the elements required by a screenplay, such as characters, plots, and themes. Book clubs, creative writing classes, and film study are also good ways to learn the basic elements of screenwriting.

Outlook

There is intense competition in the television and motion picture industries. The vast majority of writers for feature films are white males, so there are opportunities for minorities and women, especially in independent films. Employment opportunities for all writers are expected to increase about as fast as the average through 2016.

As cable television expands and digital technology allows for more programming, new opportunities for screenwriters may emerge. Television networks continue to need new material and new episodes for long-running series. Writers also will continue to find opportunities in advertising

Academy Award winning screenwriter and director, Sofia Coppola, is escorted by her brother, Roman Coppola, during an awards ceremony. (Associated Press)

agencies and educational and training video production houses.

For More Information

One of the best ways to learn about screenwriting is to read and study scripts. Read film-industry publications such as Daily Variety, Hollywood Reporter, and The Hollywood Scriptwriter.

Writers Guild of America, East
555 West 57th Street
New York, NY 10019-2925
212-767-7800
info@wgaeast.org
http://www.wgaeast.org

Writers Guild of America, West
7000 West Third Street
Los Angeles, CA 90048-4329
800-548-4532
http://www.wga.org

Secondary School Teachers

SKILLS SPOTLIGHT

What they do
Communicate ideas
Exercise leadership
Teach

Skills they need
Responsibility
Reading/writing
Speaking/listening

What Secondary School Teachers Do

Secondary school teachers instruct high school students. They usually specialize in a certain subject, such as English, mathematics, biology, or history, or they may teach several subjects. Some secondary school teachers teach specialized classes, such as information technology, business, and theater. They also inform students about colleges, occupations, and such varied subjects as the arts, health, and relationships.

In addition to classroom instruction, secondary school teachers plan lessons according to curriculum guidelines set by the school district and state. They prepare tests, grade papers, complete report cards, meet with parents, and supervise other activities. They often meet individually with students to discuss homework assignments or academic or personal problems.

Depending on the subject, teachers may use lectures, films, photographs, readings, guest speakers, discussions, or demonstrations, to name a few teaching techniques. They interact with the students and ask and answer questions to make sure everyone understands the lessons. To reinforce the material taught in class, they assign homework, give tests, and assign projects that help students develop an understanding of the material.

Each subject has its own teaching requirements. For example, science teachers supervise laboratory projects in which students work with microscopes and other equipment, and shop teachers teach students to use tools and building materials. Art teachers teach students to use paints, various sculpture media, or darkroom equipment.

Some secondary school teachers are specially trained to work with students who have disabilities. Others teach advanced lessons for students with high grades and achievement scores.

SCHOOL SUBJECTS
English, Psychology

MINIMUM EDUCATION LEVEL
Bachelor's degree

SALARY RANGE
$16,900 to $30,020 to $67,690

OUTLOOK
About as fast as the average

OTHER ARTICLES TO READ
College Professors
Elementary School Teachers
Guidance Counselors
Music Teachers
School Administrators
Special Education Teachers

A secondary school teacher tutors a student after school. (Blair Setz/Photo Researchers, Inc.)

Secondary school teachers have many responsibilities outside of the classroom as well. In between classes, they oversee study halls and supervise lunchroom activities. They attend school meetings and attend continuing education classes. Many secondary school teachers also serve as sponsors to student organizations in their field. For example, a French teacher may sponsor the French club, and a journalism teacher may advise the yearbook staff. Some secondary school teachers serve as athletic coaches or drama coaches.

Education and Training

Secondary school teachers must have at least a bachelor's degree in an approved teacher training program. You must take courses in the subject area you want to teach, as well as a number of education courses covering teaching techniques and related subjects. You must also spend several months as a student teacher under the supervision of an experienced teacher. Upon completion of the program, you receive certification as a secondary school teacher. Many teachers go on to earn master's degrees in education.

All teachers must be certified before beginning work, and many school systems require additional qualifications. While working, teachers must attend education conferences and summer workshops to maintain certification and further their training. Not all states require teachers in private or parochial schools to be licensed.

Outlook

Employment for secondary school teachers is expected to increase through 2016 to replace the large number of retiring teachers.

Other challenges for the profession involve attracting more men into teaching. The percentage of male teachers at this level continues to decline.

For More Information

Volunteer for a peer-tutoring program. Other opportunities that will give you teaching experience include coaching an athletic team at the YMCA/YWCA, counseling at a summer camp, teaching an art course at a community center, or assisting with a community theater production.

American Federation of Teachers
555 New Jersey Avenue, NW
Washington, DC 20001-2029
202-879-4400
http://www.aft.org

National Council for Accreditation of Teacher Education
2010 Massachusetts Avenue, NW, Suite 500
Washington, DC 20036-1023
202-466-7496
http://www.ncate.org

National Education Association
1201 16th Street, NW
Washington, DC 20036-3290
202-833-4000
http://www.nea.org

Secretaries

SKILL SPOTLIGHT

What they do
Communicate ideas
Help clients and customers
Manage time

Skills they need
Reading/writing
Responsibility
Speaking/listening

What Secretaries Do

Secretaries perform a variety of administrative and clerical duties. The goal of all their activities, however, is to help their employers accomplish their tasks and to help their companies conduct business in an efficient and professional manner.

Secretaries' work includes processing and transmitting information to the office staff and to other organizations. They operate office machines and arrange for their repair or servicing. These machines include computers, typewriters, dictating machines, photocopiers, switchboards, and fax machines. Secretaries order office supplies and perform regular duties such as answering phones, sorting mail, managing files, taking dictation, and writing and typing letters.

Some offices have word processing centers that handle all of the firm's typing. In these situations, *administrative secretaries* take care of all secretarial duties except for typing and dictation. This arrangement leaves them free to respond to correspondence, prepare reports, do research and present the results to their employers, and otherwise assist the professional staff. Sometimes secretaries work in groups of three or four so that they can help each other if one secretary has a heavier workload.

In many offices, secretaries make appointments for company executives and keep track of the office schedule. They make travel arrangements for the professional staff or for clients, and occasionally they are asked to travel with staff members on business trips. Other secretaries might manage the office while their supervisors are away on vacation or business trips.

Secretaries take minutes at meetings, write up reports, and compose and type letters. They often take on more responsibilities as they learn the business. Some are responsible for finding speakers for conferences, planning receptions, and arranging public relations programs. Some write copy for brochures or articles before making the arrangements to have them printed and distributed. They greet clients, guide them

SCHOOL SUBJECTS
Business, English
MINIMUM EDUCATION LEVEL
High school diploma
SALARY RANGE
$17,920 to $28,220 to $42,350
OUTLOOK
More slowly than the average

OTHER ARTICLES TO READ
Bookkeepers
Customer Service Representatives
Legal Secretaries
Receptionists
Stenographers

to the proper offices, and perform other customer service duties.

Education and Training

Secretaries need a high school education and some advanced training as well. Some students take business education classes, which include typing, shorthand, and business English. They then either look for a job or go on to college. Employers prefer hiring students who have had some technical training after high school, especially in the use of computers. Still, most clerical workers receive some on-the-job training. You can gain job experience by working part-time as a file clerk, typist, or receptionist.

Secretaries need good reading, spelling, grammatical, and mathematical skills. Many companies give exams to job applicants that test these skills.

Outlook

Employment growth for all secretaries will be slower than the average through 2016. Industries such as computer and data processing, engineering and management, and personnel supply will create the most new job opportunities.

Company downsizing and restructuring, in some cases, have redistributed traditional secretarial duties to other employees. More professionals are using personal computers to do their own corre-

Fast Fact

In the United States, about 4.2 million people work as secretaries.

spondence, but some administrative duties will still need to be handled by secretaries. Many employers complain of a shortage of capable secretaries. Those with skills and experience will have the best chances for employment. Specialized secretaries should attain certification in their field to stay competitive.

For More Information

Learn to type, and work on increasing your speed and accuracy. Volunteer to handle secretarial duties, such as typing, filing, and answering the phone at a community center, church/temple, or non-profit organization.

International Association of Administrative Professionals
PO Box 20404
10502 NW Ambassador Drive
Kansas City, MO 64195-0404
816-891-6600
service@iaap-hq.org
http://www.iaap-hq.org

Secret Service Special Agents

What Secret Service Special Agents Do

Secret Service special agents protect U.S. leaders or foreign leaders who are visiting the United States. Special agents also investigate the counterfeiting of U.S. currency. Special agents can carry and use firearms, execute warrants, and make arrests.

Today it is the Secret Service's responsibility to protect the following people: the president and vice president (also president-elect and vice president-elect) and their immediate families; former presidents and their spouses for 10 years after the president leaves office; children of former presidents until they are 16 years old; visiting heads of foreign states or governments and their spouses traveling with them, along with other distinguished foreign visitors to the United States and their spouses traveling with them; official representatives of the United States who are performing special missions abroad; major presidential and vice-presidential candidates and, within 120 days of the general presidential election, their spouses.

Special agents plan the best ways to guard the people they are assigned to protect. For example, an advance team of special agents surveys the places a protectee (the person who the Secret Service is responsible for protecting) is scheduled to visit. They identify hospitals and exit routes and work closely with local police, fire, and rescue units to develop a protection plan. They set up a command post as the communication center for protective activities. Before the protectee arrives, a lead advance agent coordinates all law enforcement representatives participating in the visit. He or she tells agents where they will be posted and notifies them about any special concerns. Just before the arrival of the protectee, agents set up checkpoints and limit access to the secure area. After the visit, special agents analyze every step

---

SCHOOL SUBJECTS
English, Foreign language, Physical education

MINIMUM EDUCATION LEVEL
Bachelor's degree

SALARY RANGE
$35,600 to $59,930 to $95,630

OUTLOOK
About as fast as the average

OTHER ARTICLES TO READ
Bodyguards
Deputy U.S. Marshals
Detectives
FBI Agents
Forensic Experts
Police Officers
Spies

---

of the operation, record unusual incidents, and suggest improvements for the future.

When Secret Service special agents are not working on a protective assignment, they investigate threats against Secret Service protectees. They also work to detect and arrest people committing any offense relating to coins, currency, stamps, government bonds, checks, credit card fraud, computer fraud, false identification crimes, and other obligations or securities of the United States.

Education and Training

Special agents must be U.S. citizens; be at least 21 at the time of appointment; have uncorrected vision no worse than 20/60 in each eye, correctable to 20/20 in each eye; pass the Treasury Enforcement Agent exam; and undergo a complete background investigation, including in-depth interviews, drug screening, medical examination, and polygraph examination.

After high school you can qualify for entry into the Secret Service by earning a four-year degree from a college or university, working for at least three years in a criminal investigative or law enforcement field, or acquiring a combination of education and experience. All newly hired agents go through nine weeks of training at the Federal Law Enforcement Training Center in Glynco, Georgia. This is followed by 11 weeks of specialized training at the Secret Service's Training Academy in Beltsville, Maryland.

Outlook

Compared to other federal law enforcement agencies, the Secret Service is small. The agency focuses on its protective missions and is not interested in expanding its responsibilities. As a result, the Secret Service will likely not grow much, unless the president and Congress decide to expand the agency's duties.

In spite of the high-alert conditions after the September 11, 2001, terrorist attacks, the Secret Service still employs a small number of people, and their new hires each year are limited. Officials anticipate that the job availability could increase slightly over the next few years.

For More Information

The Secret Service offers the Stay-In-School Program for high school students. The program allows students who meet financial eligibility guidelines to earn money by working for the agency part time, usually in a clerical position.

U.S. Secret Service
245 Murray Drive, Building 410
Washington, DC 20223-0007
202-406-5830
http://www.secretservice.gov

Secret Service agents accompany presidents and their family members, presidential candidates, and certain international political figures. Here, agents accompany Barack Obama during his 2008 presidential campaign. (Getty Images)

Security Consultants and Guards

What Security Consultants and Guards Do

Security guards keep public and private property safe from theft, vandalism, fire, and illegal entry. Sports arenas, office buildings, banks, schools, hospitals, and stores are a few of the places that security guards protect.

Other names for the various kinds of security guards are *security officers*, *patrollers*, *bouncers*, *gate tenders*, *armored-car guards*, and *airline security representatives*.

Most security guards wear some type of uniform. However, in situations where it is important for guards to blend in with the general public, they wear ordinary clothes. They might be assigned to one spot, such as at an entry to a building, where they answer people's questions, give directions, or keep possible troublemakers away. Other guards make rounds, or regular tours, of a

building or its surrounding land to make sure the property is safe and secure.

Security guards may sign visitors in and out of a building to keep track of who is in the building at any given time, direct traffic at a concert or some other type of crowded event, enforce no-smoking rules, or inspect people's packages as they come into a building. Those who are likely to encounter criminal activity in their work may carry guns.

A security guard should be healthy, alert, calm in emergencies, and able to follow directions. Good eyesight and hearing are important, too.

Security consultants do protective service work of a different kind. They develop security plans as a means of protection, and they are involved in preventing theft, vandalism, fraud, kidnapping, and other crimes.

SCHOOL SUBJECTS
Business, Psychology

MINIMUM EDUCATION LEVEL
Bachelor's degree (security consultants)
High school diploma (security guards)

SALARY RANGE
$15,880 to $22,570 to $37,850

OUTLOOK
Faster than the average

OTHER ARTICLES TO READ
Bodyguards
Border Patrol Officers
Corrections Officers
Deputy U.S. Marshals
Detectives
FBI Agents
Park Rangers
Police Officers
Secret Service Special Agents

![] Growth Field

Between 2006 and 2016 the number of security guards is expected to grow from 1,040,000 to 1,216,000, an increase of about 17 percent.

Security consultants often work with companies to help them protect their equipment and records from unwanted intruders. They study the physical conditions of a facility, observe how a company conducts its operations, and then discuss options with company officials. For example, a large company that produces military equipment may be advised to fence off its property and place electronic surveillance equipment at several points along the fence. The company may also be advised to install closed circuit television cameras and hire several security guards to monitor restricted areas. A smaller company may need only to install burglar alarms around specially restricted areas. Consultants analyze all the possibilities and then present a written proposal to management for approval.

Education and Training

Most employers prefer to hire guards who have at least a high school education. People who have had military or police experience are often considered to be good candidates for security guard jobs. Some employers may ask applicants to take sight, hearing, or aptitude tests. For some security guard jobs, experience with firearms is required. Applicants for certain guard positions may have to pass a security check, assuring that they have never been guilty of a serious crime. Security guards who work for the federal government are required to have previous military service.

Security consultants need a college degree. An undergraduate or associate's degree in criminal justice, business administration, or related field is best.

Outlook

Employment growth for guards and other security personnel is expected to be faster than the average through 2016, as crime rates rise with the overall population growth. Public concern about crime, vandalism, and terrorism continues to increase.

For More Information

Join a safety patrol at school. Volunteer to serve as a crossing guard, hall monitor, or fire monitor.

American Society for Industrial Security
1625 Prince Street
Alexandria, VA 22314-2818
703-519-6200
asis@asisonline.org
http://www.asisonline.org

Security, Police, and Fire Professionals of America
25510 Kelly Road
Roseville, MI 40866-4932
800-228-7492
http://www.spfpa.org

Semiconductor Technicians

What Semiconductor Technicians Do

Semiconductor technicians perform a variety of tasks in research laboratories to assist engineers in developing new designs for semiconductor chips. These tiny chips, often smaller than a fingernail and also called microchips, contain many miniature electronic circuits and components and are used in many kinds of modern machines.

The making of semiconductors usually begins with silicon. The silicon must be extremely pure. It is heated in furnaces and formed into cylindrical rods, which are smoothed and polished until they are perfectly round. Then they are sliced into wafers, which are processed by etching, polishing, and heat treating, to produce the desired dimensions and surface finish. After the wafers are tested, measured, and inspected, they are coated with a photosensitive substance called a photoresist.

The engineering staff prepares designs for the layout of the microchip. Technicians usually use a computer-aided design system in this work. The large computer-generated design is miniaturized as a photomask as it is applied to the silicon wafer. The photoresist then is developed in much the same manner as film in a camera, with ultraviolet light. This allows the layout of a specific microchip to be reproduced many times on the same wafer. This entire process takes place in a specially equipped clean room, free of any dust or any impurities. The tiniest speck of dust will ruin production. Next, the wafer is treated with substances that give it conducting properties. Semiconductor technicians follow the layout like a road map as they add these substances.

When this process is complete, technicians use computerized equipment that tests the many thousands of components in a matter of seconds. Many of the integrated circuits on the wafer will not function properly, and these are marked

SCHOOL SUBJECTS
Chemistry, Mathematics, Physics
MINIMUM EDUCATION LEVEL
Associate's degree
SALARY RANGE
$21,630 to $31,870 to $51,330
OUTLOOK
Decline

OTHER ARTICLES TO READ
Computer-Aided Design Technicians
Electrical and Electronics Engineers
Electronics Engineering Technicians
Hardware Engineers
Microelectronics Technicians

and discarded. After testing, the wafer is cut up into its individual chips. The chips are cased in plastic or ceramic, and metal leads are attached so they can be used in electronic circuitry. It is this final package that people refer to as a chip or semiconductor.

Semiconductor technicians are responsible for making certain that each step of the process precisely meets test specifications and also for identifying flaws and problems in the material and design. Some technicians participate in designing and building new test equipment, reporting test data, and writing production instructions for large-scale manufacture. Technicians may also be responsible for maintaining the equipment and training operators on its use.

These semiconductor technicians are working on chips that will be used in electronics. (Getty Images)

need for personnel trained in their development and processing.

Education and Training

Employers usually prefer to hire semiconductor technicians who have at least an associate's degree. Educational programs in electrical engineering technology or electronics technology are offered at junior and community colleges, technical institutes, and universities. Companies provide additional training on the specific equipment and software they use. The military can also provide a strong background in electronics.

Outlook

Employment opportunities are expected to decline through 2016 due to rising imports of computer chips and the increased automation of fabrication plants in the United States. The increasing demand for semiconductors and related devices in most areas of industry, manufacturing, and consumer services will help create a

For More Information

Join computer or electronics clubs to get hands-on learning experience with electronic circuitry.

International Society of Certified Electronics Technicians
3608 Pershing Avenue
Fort Worth, TX 76107-4527
800-946-0201
info@iscet.org
http://www.iscet.org

Semiconductor Equipment and Materials International
1401 K Street, NW, Suite 601
Washington, DC 20005-3492
202-289-0440
semidc@semi.org
http://www.semi.org

Semiconductor Industry Association
181 Metro Drive, Suite 450
San Jose, CA 95110-1344
408-436-6600
mailbox@sia-online.org
http://www.sia-online.org/home.cfm

Sheet Metal Workers

SKILLS SPOTLIGHT

What they do
Help clients or customers
Select and apply tools/technology
Work with a team

Skills they need
Mathematics
Responsibility
Speaking/listening

What Sheet Metal Workers Do

Sheet metal workers make, install, and repair rain gutters, outdoor signs, and other articles of light sheet metal, including air-conditioning, heating, and ventilation duct systems. Workers cut, bend, shape, and fasten the sheet metal to form the desired object. Sheet metal workers often work on homes and other types of construction projects.

When making an object, sheet metal workers first determine the size and type of sheet metal to use. Working from blueprints, drawings, or other instructions, they determine the measurements and angles of the object to be made. They then lay out the sheet metal and mark the pattern to be cut. In many shops, workers use computerized measuring equipment to lay out the pattern so that the least amount of metal is wasted when the pattern is cut. Workers without this equipment use tapes, rulers, and other devices to make the measurements.

Sheet metal workers do not make ducts or other objects from one piece of material. Rather, they measure and cut a number of metal pieces and then join them together to form larger sections of the finished product. Before the many pieces are joined together, workers inspect each piece to make sure it is made correctly. They then drill or punch holes into the metal and assemble the parts by welding or fastening them together.

At the construction site, workers install ducts, pipes, and other objects by joining the various parts together and securing the sections in the correct location. Workers may use hammers, pliers, or other tools to make adjustments to the objects or make some parts by hand.

Many sheet metal workers are employed by building contracting firms that construct or renovate residential, commercial, and industrial buildings. Roofing contractors, the federal government, and businesses that do their own alteration and

SCHOOL SUBJECTS
Mathematics, Physics

MINIMUM EDUCATION LEVEL
Apprenticeship

SALARY RANGE
$22,820 to $39,210 to $70,100

OUTLOOK
About as fast as the average

OTHER ARTICLES TO READ
Construction Laborers
Heating and Cooling Technicians
Layout Workers
Metallurgical Engineers and Technicians
Roofers
Welders and Welding Technicians

construction work also employ sheet metal workers. Other sheet metal workers are employed in the shipbuilding, railroad, and aircraft industries or in shops that manufacture specialty products such as custom kitchen equipment or electrical generating and distributing machinery.

Education and Training

Most apprentices in the sheet metal trade are high school graduates. Courses in algebra, geometry, trigonometry, mechanical drawing, and shop provide a good background for learning the trade.

The best way to become a sheet metal worker is to complete a four- or five-year apprenticeship program, which includes on-the-job training and classroom instruction. You can become a sheet metal worker without going through an apprenticeship program by working as a helper. However, this type of training may not be as thorough as that given to apprentices.

Outlook

Employment growth for sheet metal workers is expected to be about as fast as the average for all other occupations through 2016. Many new residential, commercial, and industrial buildings will be constructed, requiring the skills of sheet metal workers, and many older buildings will need to replace outdated heating, cooling, and ventilating systems with new energy-efficient systems. Existing equipment will need routine maintenance and repair. Dec-

Fast Fact

Sheet metal workers hold about 189,000 jobs in the United States. About 66 percent of sheet metal workers work in the construction industry.

orative sheet metal products are becoming more popular for some uses, a trend that is expected to provide an increasing amount of employment for sheet metal workers.

For More Information

Take courses such as metal shop, blueprint reading, and mechanical drawing. A summer or part-time job as a helper with a contracting firm that does sheet metal work could provide an excellent opportunity to observe workers on the job.

International Training Institute for the Sheet Metal and Air Conditioning Industry
601 North Fairfax Street, Suite 240
Alexandria, VA 22314-2083
703-739-7200
http://www.sheetmetal-iti.org

Sheet Metal and Air Conditioning Contractors' National Association
4201 Lafayette Center Drive
Chantilly, VA 20151-1209
703-803-2980
info@smacna.org
http://www.smacna.org

Sign Language Interpreters

What Sign Language Interpreters Do

Sign language interpreters help people who use sign language to communicate with people who can hear and speak English. They translate a message from spoken words to signs, and from signs to spoken words. They are fluent in American Sign Language (ASL) and/or sign systems based on English, such as Seeing Essential English, Signing Exact English, and Linguistics of Visual English.

Sign language interpreters work in hospitals and other health care facilities, for social and religious agencies, and in geriatric social work. By law, schools and businesses must make sign language interpreters available to deaf students and workers. Interpreters also work in legal settings, such as law offices and courtrooms. Others may help deaf audiences enjoy theatrical or televised performances.

Deaf interpreters translate spoken material into a language that can be understood by the deaf. This may be done in one of two ways. Sign language interpreters translate a speaker's words into ASL using their hands and fingers and then repeat aloud the deaf person's signed response to the speaker. *Oral interpreters* carefully mouth words without voicing them aloud for deaf people who can speech-read. *Tactile interpreters* work with deaf individuals who also have a visual impairment and communicate only through touch.

When interpreting, sign language interpreters must remain very visible. Interpreters must also remember that their job is to interpret only. They are not part of the conversation. Any personal asides or additions add confusion to the exchange. This professional distance is part of an established code of ethics for interpreters. This code requires confidentiality and impartiality of the interpreter. An interpreter also is responsible for educating the public about deaf issues. Anyone who plans to work as an interpreter should be aware of the code

SCHOOL SUBJECTS
English, Foreign language
MINIMUM EDUCATION LEVEL
Bachelor's degree
SALARY RANGE
$21,500 to $37,490 to $67,070
OUTLOOK
Faster than the average

OTHER ARTICLES TO READ
Court Reporters
Human Services Workers
Interpreters and Translators
Linguists
Social Workers
Special Education Teachers
Speech-Language Pathologists

A sign language interpreter signs a speech for hearing-impaired audience members as actors perform a number during a performance of the Broadway musical *Hairspray*. (Associated Press)

of ethics that has been established by the Registry of Interpreters for the Deaf (RID).

Education and Training

Many universities offer sign language training. Some also offer courses in deaf culture and have complete deaf studies programs. A college degree is not required to become a qualified interpreter, but it is a good tool to obtain better jobs and better pay.

There are two classifications of interpreters: certified and qualified. Certification by the RID is recommended, and it is required in some instances, such as in legal or courtroom situations. Qualified interpreters, with proper skills and experience, will also find a lot of work due to the shortage of interpreters.

Outlook

Sign language interpreters will be in high demand and employment opportunities are expected to grow faster than the average through 2016. There is also a growing need for relay interpreters (deaf individuals who use visual and gestural means to help other deaf people communicate). Many more deaf people are enrolling in postsecondary programs, and occupational opportunities have improved for highly educated deaf people.

For More Information

To find publications on sign language and interpreting, visit the local library, or write to the RID for its list of publications. Begin to learn ASL now—it takes many years to become an accomplished interpreter, so it pays to start your training early.

Alexander Graham Bell Association for the Deaf and Hard of Hearing
3417 Volta Place, NW
Washington, DC 20007-2737
202-337-5220 (voice)
202-337-5221 (TTY)
info@agbell.org
http://www.agbell.org

American Speech-Language-Hearing Association
2200 Research Boulevard
Rockville, MD 20850-3289
800-498-2071 (voice and TTY)
actioncenter@asha.org
http://www.asha.org

Registry of Interpreters for the Deaf
333 Commerce Street
Alexandria, VA 22314-2801
703-838-0030 (voice)
703-838-0459 (TTY)
http://www.rid.org

Singers

What Singers Do

Singers, or *vocalists*, are musicians who use musical tone, phrasing, harmony, rhythm, and melody to create vocal music.

Classical singers are usually categorized according to the range and quality of their voices, beginning with the highest singing voice, the soprano, and ending with the lowest, the bass; voices in between include mezzo-soprano, contralto, tenor, and baritone. Singers perform either alone or as members of an ensemble, or group. They may sing either with or without instrumental accompaniment; singing without accompaniment is called a cappella. In opera singers perform the various roles, much as actors, interpreting the drama with their voices to the accompaniment of a symphony orchestra.

Other professional singers perform in a certain chosen style of music, such as jazz, rock, or blues, among many others. Many singers pursue careers that will lead them to perform for coveted recording contracts, on concert tours, and for television and motion pictures. Rock, pop, country, gospel, or folk groups sing in concert halls, nightclubs, and churches and at social gatherings and for small studio recordings.

Folk singers generally perform songs that express a certain cultural tradition. Some folk singers specialize in their own or another culture, and others sing songs from a great variety of cultural and musical traditions.

Gospel singers generally sing as part of a choir, accompanied by an organ or other musical instruments, but they may also perform a cappella. Many popular singers began their careers as singers in church and gospel choirs before entering jazz, pop, blues, or rock.

Pop/rock singers perform many different styles of music, such as heavy metal, punk, rap, rhythm and blues, rockabilly, techno, and many others. Rock singers usually sing as part of a band or with a backing band to accompany them.

All singers practice and rehearse their songs and music. Some singers read from music scores while performing; others per-

SCHOOL SUBJECTS
Music, Speech
MINIMUM EDUCATION LEVEL
High school diploma
SALARY RANGE
$15,210 to $39,750 to $110,850+
OUTLOOK
About as fast as the average

OTHER ARTICLES TO READ
Composers and Arrangers
Music Conductors and Directors
Musicians
Music Teachers
Pop/Rock Musicians
Songwriters

form from memory. Yet all must gain an intimate knowledge of their music, so that they can best convey its meanings and feelings to their audience. Singers must also exercise their voices even when not performing.

Education and Training

Most singers begin learning their skills at an early age. Young children can sing in school or church choirs. Students can join concert choirs or take part in musical plays.

Most professional singers have singing teachers and voice coaches. They practice vocal exercises every day, such as scales and intervals, breath control, and diction exercises to increase the range, power, and clarity of their voices. Some colleges and universities offer music degrees with a concentration in voice.

Outlook

Competition is very strong in the music industry. Employment growth for singers, as for musicians in general, is expected to be about as fast as the average through 2016. The entertainment industry is expected to grow during the next decade, which will create jobs for singers and other performers.

For More Information

Join music clubs at school, and sing in choirs or ensembles. Many singers get their start singing in their churches at an early age. Take part in school drama productions that involve musical numbers. Audition for roles in community musical productions.

There are many summer programs offered for students interested in singing and

Bono of U2 performs to a packed house during the band's Vertigo world tour. (Landov)

other performing arts. For example, Stanford University offers a jazz workshop each summer for students who are at least 12 years old. It offers activities in instrumental and vocal music as well as swimming and other sports. For more information, contact the university at P.O. Box 20454, Stanford, CA 94309.

Boston University Tanglewood Institute
855 Commonwealth Avenue
Boston, MA 02215-1303
617-353-3350
http://www.bu.edu/cfa/music/tanglewood

National Association of Schools of Music
11250 Roger Bacon Drive, Suite 21
Reston, VA 20190-5248
703-437-0700
info@arts-accredit.org
http://www.arts-accredit.org

Opera America
330 Seventh Avenue, 16th Floor
New York, NY 10001-5010
212-796-8620
http://www.operaamerica.org

Ski Resort Workers

What Ski Resort Workers Do

Ski resorts employ a range of workers from entry level to highly skilled. All *ski resort workers* are important for maintaining the operation of the resort community. Some workers spend most of their time outdoors, while others work mostly indoors. Most ski resort employees are required to work holidays and weekends.

One of the largest departments is the ski lift operation. *Ski lift operators* are responsible for the skiers' safe transport up and down the slopes. Lift operators inspect the machinery, chairs, and loading and unloading platforms to make sure all are secure for the public. They also punch and collect lift tickets, seat passengers that need assistance, and answer any questions regarding the course, directions, or the resort in general. They must sometimes reprimand unruly passengers.

The *ski patrol* are specially trained ski experts who monitor the ski runs, the surrounding areas, and activities of the skiers. They are considered the police of the mountains and are responsible for the prevention of accidents and maintaining the safety standards of the resort. Ski patrol members help get injured skiers off the slopes to proper first-aid stations. They are skilled in emergency medical techniques, such as CPR and first aid.

Certified ski instructors teach basic maneuvers to beginning skiers as well as more advanced techniques to intermediate skiers. They hold group classes and semi-private or private lessons.

Ski technicians help outfit skiers with the necessary equipment, including the proper sized boots, skis, and poles. They answer questions regarding equipment and how it works.

Most ski resorts have chalets or lodges that offer food and entertainment. Some entry-level lodge positions include *waiters*,

SCHOOL SUBJECTS
Business, Speech
MINIMUM EDUCATION LEVEL
High school diploma
SALARY RANGE
$15,090 to $22,220 to $36,390
OUTLOOK
About as fast as the average

OTHER ARTICLES TO READ
Amusement Park Workers
Cruise Ship Workers
Gaming Workers
Recreation Workers
Resort Workers
Tour Guides

housekeeping staff, gift shop or *ski shop clerks*, and *baggage porters* and *bellhops*.

Education and Training

Education requirements for ski resort workers vary depending on the specific facility and the type of work involved. Most resorts expect their employees to be at least 18 years old and to have earned a high school diploma. Many resorts prefer to hire college students for their seasonal staff. Management positions usually require a college degree. Some colleges and universities offer a combined program of a bachelor's degree in business, economics, rehabilitation services, or general studies with a certificate concentration in the skiing industry. All ski instructors need to be certified. Workers in entry-level positions receive the bulk of their training on the job.

Outlook

Emphasis on physical health, interest in sport-related vacations, and growing household incomes point to a bright future for ski resorts and their employees.

Today many resorts use snowmaking devices to create a snow-covered run, extending the skiing season well into April. However, the majority of jobs in this industry are seasonal. Many students supplement their incomes by working at ski resorts during school vacations. Some resorts offer year-round employment by shifting their employees to other jobs in the off-season. Workers who are interested in working in the management side of the business should consider pursuing degrees in business management, rehabilitation services, or physical education.

Did You Know?

Skiing developed primarily as a means to travel from one place to another across the snow. Northern Europeans were the first people to create skis, which they made out of tree branches.

For More Information

Spend as much time on the slopes as you can. Participate in a variety of winter sports, including skiing, skating, snowmobiling, and snowboarding. Any kind of customer service experience will be valuable if you are interested in resort work.

National Ski Areas Association
133 South Van Gordon Street, Suite 300
Lakewood, CO 80228
303-987-1111
nsaa@nsaa.org
http://www.nsaa.org

Professional Ski Instructors of America
133 South Van Gordon Street, Suite 200
Lakewood, CO 80228-1706
303-987-9390
http://www.psia.org

University of Maine at Farmington
Ski Industries Certificate Program
11 South Street
Farmington, ME 04938-6823
207-778-7050
http://www.umf.maine.edu/academics/ski-industries.php?location=academics

Smokejumpers

What they do
Evaluate and manage information
Exercise leadership
Work with a team

Skills they need
Problem solving
Speaking/listening
Decision making

What Smokejumpers Do

Smokejumpers are dedicated firefighters who combat fires that threaten property and federal lands and who maintain and restore the country's forest and grassland resources. They are a special group of wildland firefighters who are dropped by parachute into remote, rugged terrain areas that are far from roads and from which access is difficult and perilous.

The concept of smokejumping was developed to quench forest fires in hard-to-reach regions. In addition to parachuting into hot spots, smokejumpers are transported by helicopters, overland transport vehicles, and by foot. Once they reach their destination, they take steps to control and put out the fire. They remain at the scene until the fire is snuffed out.

Like other firefighters, smokejumpers must be in top physical and mental shape. Their work is dangerous and physically demanding. They can often be on the fire line for 12- to 16-hour shifts for days at a time.

Although their firefighting work is seasonal, usually June through October, their efforts during this period can often be non-stop. During the off-season smokejumpers repair their gear, including the parachute rigging, and engage in physical and firefighting training activities. Smokejumpers also spend time in the off-season on non-fire activities such as trail management, brush piling, construction and facility maintenance projects.

Education and Training

At minimum, smokejumpers need a high school diploma. Courses in chemistry, English, and physical education are recommended.

Many local fire departments require education beyond high school, usually an associate's degree from an accredited fire-fighting program and training in fire-fighting skills, removal of hazardous materials, and fire prevention.

Smokejumper positions are not at the entry level. They generally require a year of

---

SCHOOL SUBJECTS
Chemistry, English, Physical education

MINIMUM EDUCATION LEVEL
High school diploma

SALARY RANGE
$18,290 to $31,420 to $61,270

OUTLOOK
Faster than the average

OTHER ARTICLES TO READ
Ecologists
Fire Control and Safety Inspectors
Firefighters
Fish and Game Wardens
Forestry Technicians
Park Rangers

Smokejumpers learn to parachute into different types of terrain as they are trained to fight forest fires. (Getty Images)

specialized fire-fighting training or two to four years of courses leading to a bachelor's degree in a discipline such as fire protection, wildland fire science, or range management. Parachuting experience is not a prerequisite.

Many smokejumpers are also certified paramedics or emergency medical technicians.

Outlook

Firefighting is expected to grow faster than the average fields so competition will be solid for openings. Smokejumper positions, in particular, will be hard to come by because of the prestige and challenge associated with this specialty area.

For More Information

Volunteer with your local fire department. You may not be old enough to work at putting out fires, but there are plenty of other ways the department can use your help. Such an experience will give you a first-hand look at what a firefighter does.

Alaska Fire Service
Bureau of Land Management
1513 Gaffney Road
Ft. Wainwright, AK 99703-1366
800-237-3658
http://www.alaskasmokejumpers.com

National Smokejumper Association
PO Box 1022
Lakeside, MT 59922-1022
406-844-0326
http://www.smokejumpers.com

U.S. Forest Service Fire and
Aviation Management
3833 South Development Avenue
Boise, ID 83705-5354
208-387-5092
http://www.fs.fed.us/fire/people/smokejumpers

Social Workers

SKILLS SPOTLIGHT

What they do
Communicate ideas
Help clients and customers
Work with a team

Skills they need
Integrity/honesty
Social
Speaking/listening

What Social Workers Do

Social workers help people with personal and community problems caused by poverty, homelessness, unemployment, illness, broken homes, family conflict, or physical, developmental, or emotional disabilities.

Most social workers meet face to face with troubled individuals or families. They work in schools to help students who have behavioral problems. They work in hospitals, helping sick people and their families adjust to the special problems caused by certain illnesses. They work in courts, police departments, and prison systems, counseling convicts, helping juvenile offenders, or assisting soon-to-be released prisoners return to life outside the jail. Social workers are employed by adoption agencies, drug and alcohol abuse programs, and agencies that help families find solutions to financial, emotional, or medical problems. They work in shelters for the homeless or for abused women and children. They also might work in nursing homes, planning social and recreational activities for the elderly.

Social workers also work with groups and may be employed by community centers, settlement houses, youth organizations, institutions for children or the elderly, hospitals, prisons, or housing projects. They provide both rehabilitation and recreational activities for groups of people with similar handicaps or problems.

Social workers who work for community organizations try to analyze the problems of an entire community and find ways to solve these problems. Juvenile delinquency, high unemployment, and high crime rates are other such problems that might require total community cooperation for a solution.

Social workers must be sensitive to people's problems and be able to handle them with a concerned, caring attitude, even if the problems make the worker sad or angry.

SCHOOL SUBJECTS
Health, Psychology

MINIMUM EDUCATION LEVEL
Bachelor's degree

SALARY RANGE
$26,380 to $45,800 to $71,940

OUTLOOK
Much faster than the average

OTHER ARTICLES TO READ
Alcohol and Drug Abuse Counselors
Geriatric Social Workers
Guidance Counselors
HIV/AIDS Counselors and Case Managers
Human Services Workers
Rehabilitation Counselors

Education and Training

To prepare for social work, you should take courses in high school that will improve your communication skills, such as English, speech, and composition. History, social studies, and sociology courses are important in understanding the concerns and issues of society.

A social worker must have a bachelor's degree in social work from an approved four-year college or university. Most students then complete at least 400 hours of supervised social work practice. Jobs with the most rewards and responsibilities go to applicants with a master's degree in social work (M.S.W.). A doctorate is required for some teaching, research, and supervisory jobs. All states require licensing, certification, or registration of social workers.

Outlook

The field of social work is expected to grow much faster than the average through 2016. This growth largely will be due to the increased number of older people who are in need of social services. Social workers who specialize in gerontology will find many job opportunities in nursing homes, hospitals, and home health care agencies.

 **Growth Field**

Between 2006 and 2016 the number of social workers is expected to grow from 595,000 to 727,000, an increase of about 22 percent.

Schools will also need more social workers to deal with issues such as teenage pregnancies, children from single-parent households, and any adjustment problems recent immigrants may have. The trend to integrate students with disabilities into the general school population will require the expertise of social workers to make the transition smoother.

Poverty is still a major issue addressed by social workers. Families are finding it increasingly challenging to make ends meet on wages that are just barely above the minimum. Working with the poor is often considered unattractive, leaving many social work positions in this area unfilled.

For More Information

Volunteer at a social service agency or community organization, or work as a counselor in a camp or summer program for children with disabilities. Your local YMCA/YWCA, park district, or other recreational facility may need volunteers for group recreation programs. Volunteer a few afternoons a week to read to people in retirement homes or to the blind.

Council on Social Work Education
1725 Duke Street, Suite 500
Alexandria, VA 22314-3457
703-683-8080
info@cswe.org
http://www.cswe.org

National Association of Social Workers
750 First Street, NE, Suite 700
Washington, DC 20002-4241
202-408-8600
info@naswdc.org
http://www.naswdc.org

Sociologists

What Sociologists Do

Sociologists study the various groups that people form. They study families, tribes, communities, and other social and political groups to understand how they develop and operate. Sociologists observe these groups and record what they find. Besides observing groups themselves, sociologists may use population counts, historical documents, and tests. To gather information, sociologists interview people or distribute questionnaires. They conduct surveys and set up experiments that place people in certain kinds of interaction. They may study how people of different races relate, how people of opposite genders communicate, and how communities are affected by different religious practices and belief systems. Lawmakers, educators, and others then use this information to help solve social problems.

A sociologist can specialize in one field. *Criminologists* study causes of crime and ways to prevent it. *Penologists* investigate punishment for crime, management of penal institutions, and rehabilitation of criminal offenders. *Social pathologists* specialize in investigation of group behavior that is considered detrimental to the proper functioning of society. *Urban sociologists* study cities and the ways people live within them. *Industrial sociologists* specialize in the relationships between employees in companies. *Clinical sociologists* study groups that do not work well or are poorly organized, and they help find ways to improve them. *Social ecologists* learn how the environment affects where and how people live. These are just a few of the many areas in which sociologists may choose to work.

Sociologists work closely with other social scientists and scientific professionals, such as statisticians, psychologists, cultural anthropologists, economists, and political scientists.

More than two-thirds of all sociologists teach in colleges and universities. They may work on sociology research projects

SCHOOL SUBJECTS
Psychology, Sociology
MINIMUM EDUCATION LEVEL
Bachelor's degree
SALARY RANGE
$36,740 to $61,140 to $108,280
OUTLOOK
About as fast as the average

OTHER ARTICLES TO READ
Anthropologists
Demographers
Economists
Historians
Parole Officers
Political Scientists
Psychologists
Social Workers

at the same time. Other sociologists work for government agencies that deal with poverty, crime, community development, and similar social problems. Sociologists also work with medical groups and physicians in the area of public health programs, which owe their effectiveness in large part to the research efforts of sociologists.

Education and Training

English, foreign languages, mathematics, science, and social studies classes will prepare you for a college sociology program. You need at least a bachelor's degree to become a sociologist. With this education, you may be able to find a job doing interviews or collecting data. With a teaching certificate, you can teach sociology in a high school. With a master's degree, you can find jobs with research institutes, industries, or government agencies. More than half of all working sociologists have doctoral degrees.

Outlook

Employment growth for sociologists is expected to be about as fast as the average through 2016. Opportunities are best for those with a doctorate and experience in fields such as demography, criminology, environmental sociology, and gerontology. Competition will be strong in all areas, however, as many sociology graduates continue to enter the job market.

As society grows older, more opportunities of study will develop for those working with the elderly. Sociologists who specialize in gerontology will have opportunities to study the aging population in a variety of environments. Sociologists will find more opportunities in marketing as companies

Fast Fact

The International Sociological Association conducted a survey to find out what its members deemed the most important sociology works of the 20th century. The top three were *Economy and Society* (Max Weber, 1922), *The Sociological Imagination* (Charles Wright Mills, 1959), and *Social Theory and Social Structure* (Robert K. Merton, 1949).

conduct research on specific populations, such as the children of baby boomers. The Internet is also opening up new areas of sociological research; sociologists, demographers, market researchers, and other professionals are studying online communities and their impact.

For More Information

Working on your school newspaper, magazine, or yearbook can help you to develop important interview, research, and writing skills as well as make you more aware of your community. Also read psychology, history, or English literature to learn about groups and human interaction.

American Sociological Association
1430 K Street, NW, Suite 600
Washington, DC 20005-2529
202-383-9005
http://www.asanet.org

Software Designers

SKILLS SPOTLIGHT
What they do
Communicate ideas
Help clients and customers
Select and apply tools/technology

Skills they need
Creative thinking
Mathematics
Problems solving

What Software Designers Do

Without software, computers would not be able to work. Software is the set of codes that tells a computer what to do. It comes in the form of the familiar packaged software that you find in a computer store, such as games, word-processing programs, spreadsheets, and desktop publishing programs. Software packages are also designed for the specific needs of a particular business. *Software designers* create these software programs, also called applications. *Computer programmers* then create the software by writing the code that gives the computer instructions.

Software designers must imagine every detail of what a software application will do, how it will do it, and how it will look on the screen. An example is how a home accounting program is created. The software designer first decides what the program should be able to do, such as balance a checkbook, keep track of incoming and outgoing bills, and keep records of expenses. For each of these tasks, the software designer decides what menus and icons to use, what each screen will look like, and whether there will be help or dialog boxes to assist the user.

Some software companies build custom-designed software for the specific needs or problems of one business. Some businesses are large enough that they employ in-house software designers who create software applications for their computer systems. These designers take into consideration the existing computer system and then work on the specific design details that are required.

Designers write a proposal outlining the design and estimating time and cost. Once approval is given, software designers and the programmers work together to write the software program. Typically, software designers write the specifications for the program, and applications programmers write the programming codes. Software designers also may be responsible for writing a user's manual or at least writing

SCHOOL SUBJECTS
Computer science, Mathematics
MINIMUM EDUCATION LEVEL
Bachelor's degree
SALARY RANGE
$39,500 to $68,080 to $109,720
OUTLOOK
Much Faster than the average

OTHER ARTICLES TO READ
Computer Programmers
Computer Systems Analysts
Database Specialists
Graphics Programmers
Quality Assurance Testers
Software Engineers
Technical Support Specialists

a report detailing what should be included in the user's manual.

Education and Training

To be a software designer, you will need a bachelor's degree in computer science plus at least one year of experience with a programming language. You also need knowledge of the field that you will be designing software for, such as education, business, or science. For example, someone with a bachelor's degree in computer science with a minor in business or accounting has an excellent chance for employment in creating business and accounting software.

Outlook

Job growth in software design is expected to be much faster than the average through 2016. Hardware designers and systems programmers are constantly developing faster, more powerful, and more user-friendly hardware and operating systems. As long as these advancements continue, the industry

Software designers work on a new program in a software development laboratory. (Scott Bauer/USDA ARS Photo Unit)

will need software designers to create software to use these improvements.

Business may have less need to contract for custom software as more prepackaged software arrives on the market that allows users with minimal computer skills to customize it according to their needs. However, the growth in the retail software market is expected to make up for this loss in customized services.

For More Information

If you are interested in computer industry careers in general, you should learn as much as possible about computers. Keep up with new technology by reading computer magazines and by talking to other computer users. Join computer clubs, and research the Internet for information about this field. Advanced students can put their design and programming knowledge to work by designing and programming simple games and utility programs.

Association for Computing Machinery
2 Penn Plaza, Suite 701
New York, NY 10121-0701
800-342-6626
acmhelp@acm.org
http://www.acm.org

IEEE Computer Society
1828 L Street, NW, Suite 1202
Washington, DC 20036
202-371-0101
http://www.computer.org

Software & Information Industry Association
1090 Vermont Avenue, NW, 6th Floor
Washington, DC 20005-4095
202-289-7442
http://www.siia.net

Software Engineers

What Software Engineers Do

Businesses use computers to do complicated work for them. In many cases, their needs are so specialized that commercial software programs cannot perform the desired tasks. *Software engineers* change existing software or create new software to solve problems in many fields, including business, medicine, law, communications, aerospace, and science.

The projects software engineers work on are all different, but their methods for solving a problem are similar. First, engineers talk to clients to find out their needs and to define the problems they are having. Next, the engineers look at the software already used by the client to see whether it could be changed or if an entirely new system is needed. When they have all the facts, software engineers use scientific methods and mathematical models to figure out possible solutions to the problems. Then they choose the best solution and prepare a written proposal for managers and other engineers.

Once a proposal is accepted, software engineers and technicians check with hardware engineers to make sure computers are powerful enough to run the new programs. The software engineers then outline program details. Engineering technicians write the initial version in computer languages.

Throughout the programming process, engineers and technicians run diagnostic tests on the program to make sure it is working well at every stage. They also meet regularly with the client to make sure they are meeting the desired goals and to learn about any changes the client wants.

When a software project is complete, the engineer prepares a demonstration of it for the client. Software engineers might also install the program, train users, and make arrangements to help with any problems that arise in the future.

Education and Training

Computer, math, and science courses will teach you fundamental skills and

SCHOOL SUBJECTS		
Computer science, Mathematics		
MINIMUM EDUCATION LEVEL		
Bachelor's degree		
SALARY RANGE		
$52,090 to $83,130 to $125,260		
OUTLOOK		
Much faster than the average		

OTHER ARTICLES TO READ
Computer Network Specialists
Computer Programmers
Database Specialists
Internet Content Developers
Internet Transaction Specialists
Quality Assurance Testers
Software Designers

Growth Field

Between 2006 and 2016 the number of software engineers is expected to grow from 857,000 to 1,181,000, an increase of about 22 percent.

analytical thinking. Classes that rely on schematic drawing and flowcharts are also very valuable.

It is strongly recommended that you earn at least an associate's degree in computer engineering or programming. Many technical and vocational schools offer a variety of programs that prepare you for a job as a software engineering technician.

A bachelor's degree is required for most software engineers. Demonstrated computer proficiency and work experience are sometimes enough to obtain a good position, but the majority of young computer professionals entering the field for the first time will be college educated. Software engineers planning to work in specific technical fields, such as medicine, law, or business, should receive some formal training in that particular discipline.

Outlook

The field of software engineering is expected to be the fastest-growing occupation through 2016. Demands made on computers increase every day and from all industries.

While the need for software engineers will remain high, computer languages will probably change every few years, and software engineers will need to attend seminars and workshops to learn new computer languages and software design. They also should read trade magazines, surf the Internet, and talk with colleagues about the field. These kinds of continuing education techniques help ensure that software engineers are best equipped to meet the needs of the workplace.

For More Information

Try to learn as much as possible about computers and computer software. Read about new developments in trade magazines, and talk to other computer users. You also can join computer clubs and surf the Internet for information about working in this field.

IEEE Computer Society
2001 L Street NW, Suite 700
Washington, DC 20036-4910
202-371-0101
http://www.computer.org

Institute for Certification of Computing Professionals
2400 Des Plaines Avenue, Suite 281
Des Plaines, IL 60018-4610
800-843-8227
http://www.iccp.org

Software & Information Industry Association
1090 Vermont Avenue, NW, 6th Floor
Washington, DC 20005-4095
202-289-7442
http://www.siia.net

Soil Conservation Technicians

SKILLS SPOTLIGHT
What they do
Communicate ideas
Evaluate and manage information
Help clients and customers

Skills they need
Mathematics
Problem solving
Reading/writing

What Soil Conservation Technicians Do

Soil conservation technicians help land users develop plans to use the soil wisely. They show farmers how to rotate their crops so that the nutrients in the soil are not exhausted. They also help foresters plan growth and harvesting cycles so that trees are not cut down before they mature.

Soil conservation technicians work mainly with farmers and agricultural concerns. They also work with land developers and local governments to prevent soil erosion and preserve wetlands.

Soil conservation technicians survey land, take soil samples, and help landowners select, install, and maintain measures that conserve and improve soil, plant, water, marsh, wildlife, and recreational resources. These measures might include contour cultivation, grass waterways, ter-racing, tree planting, field windbreaks, irrigation ditches, grass seeding, and farm drains. Other practices for soil conservation are strip cropping, tillage practices, fertilization, pesticide application, and land leveling.

Soil technicians meet with landowners to help them decide on new conservation measures or modify existing ones. They might discuss new techniques and equipment or changes in soil fertility, pesticides, and herbicides. When a soil conservationist designs a new conservation plan for a landowner, technicians inspect the different phases of the project as it is constructed. They might inspect ponds, structures, dams, tile, outlet terraces, and animal waste control facilities.

Range technicians help determine the value of rangeland, its grazing capabilities, erosion hazards, and livestock potential. *Physical science technicians* gather data in the field, study the physical characteristics of the soil, make routine chemical analyses, and set up and operate test apparatus.

SCHOOL SUBJECTS
Agriculture, Biology, Earth science
MINIMUM EDUCATION LEVEL
Bachelor's degree
SALARY RANGE
$32,750 to $56,150 to $82,080
OUTLOOK
More slowly than the average

OTHER ARTICLES TO READ
Agricultural Scientists
Foresters
Geologists
Groundwater Professionals
Range Managers
Soil Scientists

? Did You Know?

The Natural Resource Conservation Service of the U.S. Department of Agriculture was established in 1935 in response to the Dust Bowl. The Dust Bowl was caused when overplanted, nutrient-deprived land in the Plains experienced a severe drought, and the dry dirt was whipped by the winds into devastating dust storms.

Cartographic survey technicians work with cartographers (mapmakers) to map or chart the earth, survey the public domain, set boundaries, pinpoint land features, and determine the most beneficial public use. *Engineering technicians* conduct field tests and oversee some phases of construction on dams and irrigation projects. They measure acreage, place property boundaries, and define drainage areas on maps. *Surveying technicians* perform surveys for field measurement and mapping to lay out construction, check the accuracy of dredging operations, or provide reference points and lines for related work. They gather data for the design and construction of highways, dams, topographic maps, and nautical or aeronautical charts.

Education and Training

Some technical institutes and junior or community colleges offer associate's degrees in soil conservation. First-year courses in these programs include basic soils, chemistry, botany, zoology, and range management. Second-year courses include surveying, forestry, game management, fish management, and soil and water conservation.

Some soil conservation technicians hold bachelor's degrees in general agriculture, range management, crop or soil science, forestry, or agricultural engineering.

Outlook

Employment growth for conservation scientists is expected to be slower than the average through 2016. Most soil conservationists and technicians are employed by the federal government, so employment opportunities will depend in large part on levels of government spending. More opportunities may be available with state and local government agencies.

For More Information

To learn more, visit Web sites such as the Field Museum Underground Adventure (http://www.fmnh.org/ua) and the Soil Science Education Home Page (http://soil.gsfc.nasa.gov).

American Society of Agronomy
677 South Segoe Road
Madison, WI 53711
608-273-8080
http://www.agronomy.org

Natural Resources Conservation Service
U.S. Department of Agriculture
Attn: Public Affairs Division
PO Box 2890
Washington, DC 20013-2890
http://www.nrcs.usda.gov

Soil and Water Conservation Society
945 Ankeny Road, SW
Ankeny, IA 50023-9723
515-289-2331
http://www.swcs.org

Soil Scientists

What Soil Scientists Do

Soil is one of our most important natural resources. It provides the nutrients necessary to grow food for hundreds of millions of people. To use soil wisely and keep it from washing away or being damaged, experts analyze it to find the best ways to manage it. Soil scientists are these experts. They collect soil samples and study the samples' chemical and physical characteristics.

Soil scientists do much of their work outdoors. They go to fields to take soil samples. They spend many hours meeting with farmers and discussing ways to avoid soil damage. They may suggest that a farmer grow crops on different parts of a farm every few years so that the unused soil can recover. Soil scientists may also recommend that a farmer use fertilizers to put nutrients back into the soil. They may suggest ways to cover crops to keep the wind from blowing the soil away.

Soil scientists work for agricultural research laboratories, crop production companies, and other organizations. They also work with road departments to advise them about the quality and condition of the soil over which roads will be built.

All soil scientists spend time in laboratories as well as in the field. They examine soil samples under the microscope to determine bacterial and plant-food components. They also write reports based on their field notes and analyses done within the lab.

Some soil scientists specialize in one particular aspect of the work. For example, they may work as *soil mappers* or *soil surveyors*. These specialists study soil structure, origin, and capabilities through field observations, laboratory examinations, and controlled experimentation. Their investigations are aimed at determining the most suitable uses for a particular soil. *Soil fertility experts* develop practices that will increase or maintain crop size. They consider both the type of soil and the crop planted in their analysis. Various soils react differently when exposed to fertilizers, soil additives, crop rotation, and other farming techniques.

SCHOOL SUBJECTS
Agriculture, Biology, Earth science

MINIMUM EDUCATION LEVEL
Bachelor's degree

SALARY RANGE
$34,620 to $58,000 to $100,800

OUTLOOK
More slowly than the average

OTHER ARTICLES TO READ
Agricultural Scientists
Farmers
Foresters
Horticultural Technicians
Range Managers
Soil Conservation Technicians

Education and Training

The best way to become a soil scientist is to go to college and earn a bachelor's degree. Then you should go on to earn a master's degree in agricultural science. A degree in biology, physics, or chemistry would also qualify you for employment as a soil scientist, but you should take some courses in agriculture. With a bachelor's degree in agricultural science, you can get some non-research jobs, but most research and teaching positions require a doctorate.

Outlook

Employment growth in soil science is expected to be slower than the average through 2016. Growth in this field is affected by the government's involvement in farming studies—if federal and state budgets are cut, it will limit funding for this type of job. However, private businesses will continue to demand soil scientists for research and sales positions. Companies dealing with seed, fertilizers, or farm equipment are examples of private industries that hire soil scientists.

Technological advances in equipment and methods of conservation will allow scientists to better protect the environment as well as improve farm production. Scientists' ability to evaluate soils and plants will improve with more precise research methods.

❓ Did You Know?

The U.S. Department of Agriculture (USDA) was created in 1862 to give farmers information about new crops and improved farming techniques. Although this department started small, today it is one of the largest agencies of the federal government.

For More Information

Contact your local branch of the National FFA Organization (http://www.ffa.org) or 4-H club (http://www.fourhcouncil.edu) or your county's soil conservation department to learn about regional projects.

American Society of Agronomy
677 South Segoe Road
Madison, WI 53711-1086
608-273-8080
http://www.agronomy.org

National Society of Consulting Soil Scientists
PO Box 1724
Sandpoint, ID 83864-0901
800-535-7148
info2008@nscss.org
http://www.nscss.org

Soil Science Society of America
677 South Segoe Road
Madison, WI 53711-1086
608-273-8080
http://www.soils.org

Solar Engineers

SKILLS SPOTLIGHT

What they do
Help clients and customers
Work with a team
Create or improve systems

Skills they need
Problem solving
Mathematics
Creative thinking

What Solar Engineers Do

Efficient use of "green technologies" is a key topic in any discussion about energy today. Green technology, or clean technology, is the concept of applying environmental science to safeguard our planet by lessening the negative effect of human activity. Such green technologies as solar energy, bio fuels, and wind power serve as alternatives to fossil fuels—nonrenewable energy forms that harm Earth.

Solar energy employs photovoltaic, commonly known as PV, systems to draw nonpolluting energy from the sun. *Solar engineers* apply principles of biology, chemistry, and mathematics to produce energy for homes, businesses, and commercial properties that use solar power for electricity and heat. They design and develop systems that provide energy in a manner that is economical as well as environmentally safe.

Solar engineers study the impact of the sun's energy on the environment, in particular its effect on global warming and ozone depletion. Some engineers are self-employed, independent consultants who provide information to clients about regulations and new solar technology designs and developments.

In addition to solar energy, today's engineers use their knowledge of the many different closely integrated green technologies to provide a suite of energy-saving sources to produce zero-energy designs and whole-building integration.

Education and Training

To prepare for a career in engineering, take as many high school courses as you can in the physical sciences and mathematics. Computer courses, such as computer-aided design and drafting, will provide you with basic knowledge in engineering software programs.

In general, entry-level engineering positions require a bachelor's degree in an engineering specialty; some research jobs

---

SCHOOL SUBJECTS
Chemistry, Biology, Mathematics

MINIMUM EDUCATION LEVEL
Bachelor's degree

SALARY RANGE
$43,180 to $69,940 to $106,230

OUTLOOK
About as fast as the average

OTHER ARTICLES TO READ
Civil Engineers and Civil Engineering
   Technicians
Electrical and Electronics Engineers
Environmental Engineers
Mechanical Engineers

This solar engineer checks the solar panels on the roof of the Field Museum of Natural History in Chicago, Illinois. (Getty Images)

may require a master's degree. A few colleges offer degrees in solar energy engineering, but solar engineers may also pursue environmental engineering as their area of concentration.

Engineering degree programs focus heavily on mathematics and the physical and life sciences.

Most engineering positions require practitioners to be licensed. Employers favor those taking continuing education courses as this ensures their workers are up-to-date with the changing technology.

Outlook

Job opportunities for engineers are expected to grow about as the fast as the average, but may vary by area of concentration.

While the current focus on sustainable energy is producing more environmental engineers, including solar engineers, the market should not be saturated, as many opportunities exist in this specialized field. Among them is the need for research of new designs and their implementation.

For More Information

Visit the Junior Engineering and Technical Society's Web site (http://www.jets.org) to learn more about opportunities in solar engineering. In particular, read articles in JETS's publication *Pre-Engineering Times* about this specialty engineering area.

ABET, Inc.
111 Market Place, Suite 1050
Baltimore, MD 21202-7116
410-347-7700
http://www.abet.org

American Society for Engineering Education
1818 N Street, NW, Suite 600
Washington, DC 20036-2479
202-331-3500
http://www.asee.org

National Society of Professional Engineers
1420 King Street
Alexandria, VA 22314-2750
703-684-2800
http://www.nspe.org

North American Board of Certified Energy Practitioners
10 Hermes Road, Suite 400
Malta, NY 12020-4483
800-654-0021
info@nabcep.org
http://www.nabcep.org

Songwriters

SKILLS SPOTLIGHT

What they do
Communicate ideas
Exercise leadership
Help clients and customers

Skills they need
Creative thinking
Self-esteem
Reading/writing

What Songwriters Do

Songwriters write the words and sometimes the music for songs, including songs for recordings, advertising jingles, and theatrical performances. They may also perform these songs. Songwriters who write only the words and not the music are called *lyricists*.

Songwriters may choose to write about emotions, such as love or sadness. They put their ideas into a small number of words, focusing on the sounds of the words together. Many songwriters carry a notebook and write about things that they hear or see. They may write songs about people, events, or experiences. They may write about broad themes that will be understood by everyone, drawing ideas from current events or social situations such as poverty, racial issues, or war. Or they may write about personal issues, based on their own experiences or conversations with others.

Songwriters usually have a musical style in mind when they write lyrics. These styles include pop, rock, hip-hop, rap, country, blues, jazz, and classical.

Songwriters who work for advertising agencies write about certain products for radio and television commercials. Producers also hire songwriters to write lyrics for operas, Broadway shows, or movies.

Many songwriters have a certain method for writing songs. Sometimes they write the title first because it allows them to capture a theme in just a few words. Many songwriters find that there are about four common characteristics found in a song: an identifiable, universal idea; a memorable title; a strong beginning; and an appropriate form, including rhythm, verse, and refrain.

The development of a song can be a highly collaborative process between a lyricist and a composer. The composer might play a few measures on an instrument, and the lyricist tries to write words that fit well with the music. Or the lyricist suggests a few words or lines and the composer tries to write music that fits the words.

SCHOOL SUBJECTS
Music, Speech
MINIMUM EDUCATION LEVEL
High school diploma
SALARY RANGE
$16,110 to $40,150 to $111,490
OUTLOOK
About as fast as the average

OTHER ARTICLES TO READ
Composers and Arrangers
Music Conductors and Directors
Musicians
Music Producers
Music Teachers
Pop/Rock Musicians
Singers

Songwriters, composers, and other musicians often use MIDI (musical instrument digital interface) technology to produce sounds through synthesizers, drum machines, and samplers. These sounds are usually controlled by a computer, and the composer or songwriter can mix, alter, and refine the sounds using mixing boards and computer software.

Education and Training

Songwriters must have a good understanding of language and grammar. Courses in English composition, poetry, music theory, and journalism will be helpful. Learning how to play a musical instrument is a good idea, particularly the guitar or a keyboard instrument, since these instruments help you understand melody, harmony, and chord structures. Music theory, ear-training, and composition classes will teach you to write accurate musical notation.

There is really no formal training that a songwriter must have to write songs. Songwriting workshops sometimes are offered by community colleges and music schools. College music programs offer intensive studies in music history, theory, and performance, and they expose you to a variety of musical styles.

Outlook

Most songwriters are unable to support themselves from their songwriting alone and must hold other part-time or full-time jobs while writing songs in their spare time. The competition in this industry is extremely intense, and there are many more songwriters than paying projects. This situation is expected to continue into the next decade.

Songwriter John Legend is working on his album in a recording studio in Atlanta, Georgia. (WireImage/Getty Images)

For More Information

Learn to play a musical instrument, especially the piano or guitar. Start writing your own songs, and experiment with melody and lyrics. Most schools and communities have orchestras, bands, and choruses that offer opportunities to explore music.

American Society of Composers, Authors, and Publishers
One Lincoln Plaza
New York, NY 10023-7129
212-621-6000
http://www.ascap.com

National Association of Composers/USA
PO Box 49256, Barrington Station
Los Angeles, CA 90049-0256
818-247-6048
http://www.music-usa.org/nacusa

Songwriters Guild of America
1560 Broadway, Suite 408
New York, NY 10036-1518
212-768-7902
ny@songwritersguild.com
http://www.songwritersguild.com

Special Education Teachers

SKILLS SPOTLIGHT

What they do
Communicate ideas
Teach
Work with a team

Skills they need
Reading/writing
Responsibility
Speaking/listening

What Special Education Teachers Do

Special education teachers work with students who need special attention, including those who have physical, developmental, behavioral, or learning disabilities as well as those who are gifted and talented. They create individual programs for each student, called an Individualized Education Program (IEP). An IEP sets personalized goals for a student, based upon his or her learning style and ability, and it outlines specific steps to prepare him or her for employment or postsecondary schooling. Special education teachers work closely with students to determine their learning and skill levels, and they work with school psychologists, social workers, occupational and physical therapists, and speech-language therapists.

Some students have learning disabilities that prevent them from learning through usual teaching methods. They may need instruction at a slower pace or to work in quiet, nondistracting settings. Teachers may need to read assignments aloud to them and help them focus their attention on schoolwork.

Some students have emotional or behavioral problems. Others are considered below average in their mental abilities. Some students are language impaired, which means they have trouble communicating. Special education teachers work with students who are visually impaired, hard of hearing, or deaf. They also help students with physical handicaps such as muscle, nerve, or bone disorders. When working with physically handicapped students, teachers may use special equipment, such as computers that are operated by touching a screen or by voice commands or books in Braille.

The current trend in education is to integrate students with disabilities into regular classrooms to the extent that it is

SCHOOL SUBJECTS
English, Speech

MINIMUM EDUCATION LEVEL
Bachelor's degree

SALARY RANGE
$33,930 to $49,640 to $78,900

OUTLOOK
Faster than the average

OTHER ARTICLES TO READ
Elementary School Teachers
English as a Second Language Teachers
Preschool Teachers
Secondary School Teachers
Teacher Aides

possible and beneficial to them. This is often called "mainstreaming" or "inclusion." Mainstreaming requires special education teachers to work with general education teachers in general education classrooms. They help adapt curriculum materials and teaching techniques to meet the needs of students with disabilities and offer guidance to teachers on dealing with students' emotional and behavioral problems.

Most special education teachers work in public schools. Some, however, work in local education agencies, colleges and universities, and private schools.

Education and Training

College preparatory courses in English, science, math, and government will help you prepare for this career. Speech courses will develop good communication skills, and psychology courses will help you understand some of the learning problems your students face.

The requirements for becoming a special education teacher are similar to those for becoming an elementary or secondary school teacher, but meeting them may involve a longer period of training. All states require teachers to earn a bachelor's degree that includes specific education courses. Many states require an additional year or two of graduate study, and some states require a master's degree in special education. You also must be certified by your state.

Outlook

The field of special education is expected to grow faster than the average through 2016. This demand is caused partly by the growth in the number of special education students who need services. Medical advances resulting in more survivors of illness and accidents and the rise in birth defects due to women bearing children in later years, as well as general population growth, are all significant factors leading to a demand for these educators.

For More Information

Get to know special-needs students at your school. Learn to use sign language or read Braille. To learn more about disability issues, visit this Web site with links to a variety of resources: http://disabilitystudies.syr.edu/resources/otherdisabilityresources.aspx. Also visit Ragged Edge online, a magazine that covers the disability experience in America: http://www.ragged-edge-mag.com.

Council of Administrators of Special Education
Osigian Office Center
101 Katelyn Circle, Suite E
Warner Robbins, GA 31088-6484
478-333-6892
lpurcell@bellsouth.net
http://www.casecec.org

National Education Association
1201 16th Street, NW
Washington, DC 20036-3290
202-833-4000
http://www.nea.org

 **Growth Field**

Between 2006 and 2016 the number of special education teachers is expected to grow from 459,000 to 530,000, an increase of about 15 percent.

Special Effects Technicians

What Special Effects Technicians Do

Special effects technicians make fantastic things seem real in movies, theater, and television. They can make a spaceship fly to distant planets, perch a car on top of a skyscraper, or bring dinosaurs to life on the screen.

Special effects technicians read scripts and meet with directors to decide on the kinds of effects they will use. There are several trades that make up special effects, and special effects companies, known as shops, may do business in one or several of these trades. The services they may offer include mechanical effects, computer animation, makeup effects, and pyrotechnics.

Mechanical effects specialists build sets, props, and backgrounds for film, television, and theater productions. They build, install, and operate equipment mechanically or electrically. They usually are skilled in carpentry, electricity, welding, and robotics.

Computer animation specialists use computer programs to create effects that would be impossible or too costly to build. These effects make it possible for a human face to change or "morph" into an animal's face, or for a realistic-looking bear to drink a popular soda. Computer technology is advancing rapidly. Most films in the adventure and horror categories make extensive use of computer animation, but it is also used today in every other type of filmmaking.

Makeup effects specialists create masks and costumes. They build prosthetic devices, such as human or animal heads or limbs. They are skilled at modeling, sewing, applying makeup, and mixing dyes.

Pyrotechnics effects specialists are experts with firearms and explosives. They create explosions for dramatic scenes. This work can be very dangerous. Most states require them to be licensed to handle and set off explosives.

Many special effects technicians work freelance, so there can be long periods of no work (and no pay) between jobs.

SCHOOL SUBJECTS
Chemistry, Computer science
MINIMUM EDUCATION LEVEL
Some postsecondary training
SALARY RANGE
$30,620 to $54,550 to $98,050
OUTLOOK
About as fast as the average

OTHER ARTICLES TO READ
Cartoonists and Animators
Cinematographers
Film and Television Producers
Lighting Technicians
Stage Production Workers
Stunt Performers

Fast Fact

Computer generated imagery (CGI) in movies has taken huge technological leaps from early fare such as *Tron* (1982). The latest in CGI has appeared in films such as *The Lord of the Rings* movies and *The Curious Case of Benjamin Button* (2008).

Education and Training

To be a special effects technician, you need to know about science and art. Take classes in art, art history, sculpture, chemistry, physics, shop, and computers.

Some universities have film and television programs that offer courses in special effects. Some special effects technicians major in theater, art history, photography, and related subjects. Some of the computer animation technicians working today have not had any special schooling or training but have mastered graphics programs on their own.

Most technicians in the industry say that the best way into this career is through experience working on a film crew.

Outlook

Employment opportunities for artists and related workers, including special effects technicians, is expected to grow about as fast as the average through 2016, but the competition for jobs in film special effects houses is fierce. For more than 20 years now, films of all genres have incorporated computer graphics and high-tech effects, inspiring a whole generation of young people with computers and imaginations.

Digital technology will continue to rapidly change the industry. Experts predict that within the next decade, film will be eliminated and movies will be shot and projected digitally, enhancing computer effects. Filmmakers will edit their movies over the Internet.

For More Information

Work on school drama productions as a stagehand, sound technician, or makeup artist. You will learn about set and prop design and how to use tools and mechanical and electrical equipment. Explore computer animation software programs that allow you to create special effects.

American Film Institute
2021 North Western Avenue
Los Angeles, CA 90027-1657
323-856-7600
http://www.afi.com

Animation World Network
6525 Sunset Boulevard, Garden Suite 10
Los Angeles, CA 90028-7212
323-606-4200
info@awn.com
http://www.awn.com

Visual Effects Society
5535 Balboa Boulevard, Suite 205
Encino, CA 91316-1544
818-981-7861
info@VisualEffectsSociety.com
http://www.visualeffectssociety.com

Special Procedures Technologists

What Special Procedures Technologists Do

Special procedures technologists operate medical diagnostic imaging equipment such as computed tomography (CT) and magnetic resonance imaging (MRI) scanners. They assist in imaging procedures such as angiography and cardiac catheterization. They work in various health care settings, such as hospitals, clinics, and imaging centers.

Special procedures technologists assist radiologic technologists with positioning patients for examination, immobilizing them, preparing the equipment, and monitoring the equipment and patients' progress during procedures. An *angiographer* is a special procedures technologist who assists with a procedure called an angiogram, which shows any changes that may have occurred to the blood vessels of the patient's circulatory system.

Some special procedures technologists assist cardiologists with a procedure called cardiac catheterization. They monitor and document the patients' vital signs, such as blood pressure and respiration, and they enter that information directly into a computer that controls testing procedures.

Some special procedures technologists assist with CT scanning (also known as CAT scanning), which combines X rays with computer technology to create images that provide more details than standard X rays. The technologist observes and reassures patients while testing procedures are performed.

Another imaging procedure called magnetic resonance imaging (MRI) produces the most detailed and flexible images of all the various imaging techniques. A special procedures technologist often assists with this procedure by explaining the test to the patient and making certain that the patient is not carrying any metal objects that could be hazardous to the patient during the test and could also damage the equipment. The MRI technologist enters necessary data into

SCHOOL SUBJECTS
Biology, Chemistry

MINIMUM EDUCATION LEVEL
Associate's degree

SALARY RANGE
$42,250 to $59,860 to $81,260

OUTLOOK
Faster than the average

OTHER ARTICLES TO READ
Cardiovascular Technologists
Diagnostic Medical Sonographers
Electroneurodiagnostic Technologists
Nuclear Medicine Technologists
X-ray Technologists

Growth Field

Between 2006 and 2016 the number of special procedures technologists is expected to grow about 15 percent.

a computer, such as patient information, the orientation of the scan, and the part of the body to be scanned. The technologist might initiate the scan and observe the patient through a window in the control room and on a closed-circuit video display while maintaining voice contact and reassuring the patient.

Education and Training

After receiving a high school diploma, you must attend a two-year program and earn an associate's degree in radiology. These degree programs are offered at community colleges, vocational and technical training schools, or in the military. Most radiology technologists receive training through a program accredited by the American Medical Association's Committee on Allied Health Education and Accreditation.

Outlook

Employment growth for radiologic technologists, including special procedures technologists, will be faster than the average through 2016. As the population ages and heart disease and cancer continue to be among the primary health concerns in the United States, there will continue to be a high demand for skilled technologists who can assist in the diagnosis, prevention, and treatment of these and other conditions.

For More Information

Volunteer work at a hospital, nursing home, or other medical facility can give you experience working with patients and medical professionals in a health care environment.

American Registry of Radiologic Technologists
1255 Northland Drive
St. Paul, MN 55120-1155
651-687-0048
http://www.arrt.org

American Society of Radiologic Technologists
15000 Central Avenue, SE
Albuquerque, NM 87123-3909
800-444-2778
http://www.asrt.org

Joint Review Committee on Education in Radiologic Technology
20 North Wacker Drive, Suite 2850
Chicago, IL 60606-3182
312-704-5300
mail@jrcert.org
http://www.jrcert.org

Speech-Language Pathologists

What Speech-Language Pathologists Do

Speech-language pathologists, or *speech therapists*, use tests to identify speech disorders in people and then try to help them overcome speech difficulties.

Clients of speech-language pathologists include people who cannot make speech sounds or cannot make them clearly; people who have speech rhythm and fluency problems, such as stuttering; people with voice quality problems, such as inappropriate pitch or harsh voice; people who have problems understanding and producing language; and people with cognitive communication impairments, such as attention, memory, and problem-solving disorders. Speech-language pathologists may also work with people who have oral motor problems that cause eating and swallowing difficulties. Clients' problems may be caused by hearing loss, brain injury or deterioration, cerebral palsy, stroke, cleft palate, voice pathology, mental retardation, or emotional issues.

Speech-language pathologists conduct written and oral tests and use special instruments to analyze and diagnose the impairment. They develop an individualized treatment plan, which may include automated devices and sign language. They teach clients how to make sounds, improve their voices, or increase their language skills to communicate more effectively.

Most therapists work in schools, where they test students regularly for speech disorders. The students who have speech problems either receive therapy at the school or go to a speech clinic for treatment. At a clinic, they receive physical therapy and help from psychologists. Sometimes, speech pathologists teach patients to develop entirely new speech skills using tongue exercises and speech drills.

SCHOOL SUBJECTS
Biology, Speech
MINIMUM EDUCATION LEVEL
Master's degree
SALARY RANGE
$40,200 to $60,690 to $94,740
OUTLOOK
About as fast as the average

OTHER ARTICLES TO READ
Linguists
Physicians
Psychologists
Rehabilitation Counselors
Sign Language Interpreters
Social Workers
Special Education Teachers

Speech therapy can be given either individually or in groups. Usually, patients feel more comfortable when they work alone with a therapist. However, some people make more progress when they are placed with people who have similar speech problems.

Education and Training

To become a speech pathologist, you must earn a college degree. Most states require that pathologists have a master's degree in speech-language pathology before they can apply for a job. Undergraduate courses usually include the study of the body (anatomy), psychology, biology, physiology, and the study of speech and languages (linguistics, semantics, and phonetics).

If you want to work as a speech therapist in a public school, you must earn a teacher's certificate and pass the state requirements for working with children with disabilities. Most states require some type of licensing or registration for speech-language pathologists, and 14 states require all speech-language pathologists to be licensed, regardless of work setting.

Outlook

Employment growth for speech-language pathologists will be about as fast as the average through 2016. The job outlook depends on economic factors, further budget cutbacks by health care providers and insurance companies, and legal requirements for services for people with disabilities.

Nearly half of the new jobs emerging are expected to be in speech and hearing clinics, physicians' offices, and outpatient care facilities. Substantial job growth will continue to occur in elementary and secondary schools because of laws that guar-

Fast Fact

Stuttering is the most common speech defect. Speech therapy can often help this problem. According to the Stuttering Foundation of America, more than three million Americans stutter.

antee special education and related services to minors with disabilities.

Many new jobs will be created in hospitals, nursing homes, rehabilitation centers, and home health agencies; most of these openings will probably be filled by private practitioners employed on a contract basis.

For More Information

Begin to learn sign language. Volunteer to work in clinics and hospitals or in speech, language, and hearing centers. Participate in a speech club to practice oral speaking skills. Voice training, either speaking or singing, will teach you about creating and controlling vocal sounds.

American Auditory Society
352 Sundial Ridge Circle
Dammeron Valley, UT 84783-5196
435-574-0062
http://www.amauditorysoc.org

American Speech-Language-Hearing Association
2200 Research Boulevard
Rockville, MD 20850-3289
301-296-5700
actioncenter@asha.org
http://www.asha.org

# Speechwriters

SKILLS SPOTLIGHT
What they do
Communicate ideas
Evaluate and manage information
Help clients and customers

Skills they need
Creative thinking
Reading/writing
Speaking/listening

What Speechwriters Do

Speechwriters prepare speeches for politicians in all branches of government, from the local and state level to the national level, including the president of the United States, or they may write speeches for business professionals.

Many politicians and business executives are extremely busy and do not have time to write the speeches they need to give. Others may not feel comfortable writing their own speeches and require a speechwriter to help them make sense of what they want to say, and how they want to convey that message in a speech. Still others may have excellent ideas for their speeches but need help communicating their vision to others.

A speechwriter usually begins writing a speech once a topic is selected. The topic may be assigned to them, or they may have to determine the topic themselves. To do this, a speechwriter may meet with the person they are writing for to receive his or her suggestions. Next, the speechwriter will research the topic to be discussed in the speech, using the resources of libraries, the Internet, or interviews with knowledgeable authorities in the field.

Once a speechwriter has gathered enough initial information, they begin to write the speech. Speechwriters need to make sure the speech sounds like it was written by the person who will deliver it. They also need to keep in mind who will be hearing the speech, making sure that the speech is written in a way that it will be understood by the intended audience, and that it will be effective relating the intended message. They also have to be sure the speech does not exceed specified time limits.

After the speech is approved (which can take several rounds of drafts and suggestions), the speechwriter may be responsible for producing the speech in its final form, which varies depending on the situations. The speech may need to be typed on note cards for someone speaking in a small auditorium, or the speech might need to be on a computer disk that can be input into a TelePrompTer and displayed on a monitor

SCHOOL SUBJECTS
English, Government, Speech
MINIMUM EDUCATION LEVEL
Bachelor's degree
SALARY RANGE
$29,580 to $49,800 to $94,620
OUTLOOK
About as fast as the average

OTHER ARTICLES TO READ
Copywriters
Political Columnists and Writers
Political Reporters
Reporters
Writers

A speechwriter brainstorms ideas with officials. (Corbis)

for the person to read at a large rally, meeting, or televised event.

Successful speechwriters stay up-to-date with current events and daily news. They work under pressure to meet deadlines. Because speechwriters need to interact with others, they have good people skills.

Education and Training

Since speechwriters need to be strong communicators, you should take as many English, speech, and communications courses as you can. Take courses in civics, history, and government as well. You also will need a bachelor's degree, preferably in a field related to communications. To become a speechwriter for politicians, you will probably want to pursue a degree in political science.

Outlook

Employment opportunities for writers of all types, including speechwriters, are expected to grow about as fast as the average through 2016. Given the importance of effective communication in the world today, it may be correct to assume that speechwriters in all fields will have steady employment opportunities for the next decade.

For More Information

You can practice writing speeches on your own, or you can participate with your school's speech or debate teams. Reading famous speeches will also help you to understand the components of a successful speech. You can also join nonprofit or political organizations and offer to assist with public speaking events. This will give you the opportunity to make contacts, observe their operations, and perhaps get an opportunity to assist a speechwriter with research.

American Association of Political Consultants
600 Pennsylvania Avenue, SE, Suite 330
Washington, DC 20003-6300
202-544-9815
info@theaapc.org
http://www.theaapc.org

Toastmasters International
PO Box 9052
Mission Viejo, CA 92690-9052
949-858-8255
http://www.toastmasters.org

Spies

SKILLS SPOTLIGHT

What they do
Communicate ideas
Evaluate and manage information
Select and apply tools/technology

Skills they need
Creative thinking
Reading/writing
Speaking/listening

What Spies Do

Spies, also called *intelligence officers*, work for the U.S. government to gather information about the governments of foreign countries. This information, called intelligence, is one of the tools the U.S. government uses to help make decisions about its own military, economic, and political policies. Intelligence may include political, economic, military, scientific, technical, geographic, and other types of information, both public and secret.

There are two types of intelligence officers, *case officers* and *analysts*. Case officers, also called *operators*, are most often involved in the colorful and dangerous sorts of activities shown in the movies. They collect intelligence, usually in foreign countries. Ways of gathering information can be as open (overt) as reading a foreign newspaper or as complicated and secret (covert) as eavesdropping on a telephone conversation. Sources of intelligence include foreign radio and television broadcasts, public documents, interviews with tourists,

air surveillance, and camera-loaded satellites. Aerial and space reconnaissance, electronic eavesdropping, and agent espionage are considered covert sources.

Analysts are more likely to be stationed in an office in Washington, D.C., although some also work abroad. They interpret and analyze data they have received from case officers and other sources. *Technical analysts* gather data from satellites. *Cryptographic technicians* are experts at encoding, decoding, and sending secret messages.

There are three categories of intelligence operations: strategic, tactical, and counter-intelligence. People working in strategic intelligence keep track of world events, watch foreign leaders very carefully, and study a foreign country's politics, economy, people, military operations, and any scientific advances it may be making. Intelligence can be "hard" or "soft." Hard intelligence is quantifiable and verifiable—for example, military and technological information such as the number of active

SCHOOL SUBJECTS
Government, History

MINIMUM EDUCATION LEVEL
Bachelor's degree

SALARY RANGE
$35,600 to $59,930 to $95,630

OUTLOOK
Faster than the average

OTHER ARTICLES TO READ
Cryptographic Technicians
Customs Officials
FBI Agents
Foreign Service Officers
Police Officers
Political Scientists
Secret Service Special Agents

troops in Libya. An example of soft intelligence would be attempting to predict who will be the next leader of Bolivia.

Tactical intelligence gathering involves collecting the same kind of information, but in combat areas and risky political settings abroad. Counter-intelligence officers protect U.S. secrets, institutions, and intelligence activities. They identify and prevent enemy operations that might hurt the United States, its citizens, or its allies. Such enemy plots include worldwide terrorism and drug trafficking.

Education and Training

All of the federal intelligence services look for people of high moral character, excellent academic records, and sincere patriotic commitment. Applicants must be U.S. citizens and at least 21 years old. You must earn a bachelor's degree, and an advanced degree is required for some positions. Specialized skills, computer knowledge, and fluency in foreign languages are also important.

Outlook

Intelligence operations are closely linked to the world political situation. In general, people with specialized skills or backgrounds in the languages and customs of certain countries will continue to be in high demand. The outlook on intelligence jobs remains good, and new officers will be hired every year. The United States has become focused on terrorist activity, particularly from groups based in the Middle East, and it remains concerned with the spread of nuclear, chemical, and biological weapons; the environment; and worldwide human health. Intelligence has become one of the world's largest industries; in the United States alone, it is supported by a multibillion-dollar annual budget.

For More Information

Ask your librarian to help you find books about famous spies throughout American history. Visit the CIA Kids Home Page at https://www.cia.gov/kids-page/index.html to learn more about the CIA and intelligence gathering.

Central Intelligence Agency
Office of Public Affairs
Washington, DC 20505-0001
703-482-0623
http://www.odci.gov

Defense Intelligence Agency
200 MacDill Boulevard
Civilian Personnel Division (DAH-2)
Washington, DC 20340-5100
202-231-8228
staffing@dia.mil
http://www.dia.mil

U.S. Department of State
Public Communication Division
PA/PL, Room 2206
2201 C Street, NW
Washington, DC 20520-0001
202-647-6575
http://www.state.gov

 Did You Know?

The infamous spy Mata Hari (born Margaretha Geertruida Zelle in The Netherlands) was accused by the French government of spying for Germany during World War I. She was put on trial, found guilty, and was executed by firing squad in 1917.

Sporting Goods Production Workers

What Sporting Goods Production Workers Do

Team sports and personal physical fitness have come to enjoy widespread popularity in the last decade. Professional and college sports teams dominate radio and television and the sports pages of newspapers. At the amateur level, health and racquet-sports clubs have become common sources of recreation for many people who live in the United States.

This sports and fitness boom has increased the demand for a wide variety of sports equipment, ranging from tennis and bowling balls to hockey and lacrosse sticks. *Sporting goods production workers* operate the machinery that makes this sports equipment. In addition, many of these workers hand-make equipment that cannot be produced by machines.

Many sporting goods production workers are *machine operators*. The machines they operate range from sewing machines to large, complex automated equipment. These machines heat, mold, stretch, cut, pound, and trim the materials that are used in the production of sporting equipment.

Assemblers are workers who put together the parts of products. These workers clean, paint, polish, stitch, weave, lace, glue, weld, or engrave objects. *Floor assemblers* work with power tools and large, automated machines. *Bench assemblers* do more exacting work, putting together small parts and testing finished products. *Precision assemblers* perform tasks that require special skills. These workers sometimes test new designs and products.

Many sporting goods production workers' tasks are highly specialized. These specialized workers include *hand baseball sewers*, *golf club assemblers*, *base fillers and stuffers*, *baseball glove shapers*, *inflated ball molders*, and *bowling ball engravers*.

SCHOOL SUBJECTS
Physical education, Technical/Shop

MINIMUM EDUCATION LEVEL
High school diploma

SALARY RANGE
$21,370 to $32,550 to $48,050

OUTLOOK
More slowly than the average

OTHER ARTICLES TO READ
Plastics Products Manufacturing Workers
Precision Machinists and Metalworkers
Toy Industry Workers

Some sporting goods production workers do custom work, meaning that they produce equipment one piece at a time by hand and with special smaller machines. For instance, a worker may produce custom-made ice skates for professional hockey players or Olympic figure skaters.

Most team sports have strict rules and regulations regarding the size and shape of equipment as well as the materials used in manufacturing it. Quality-control inspectors make sure that all manufactured equipment conforms to these rules and regulations.

This worker is using a machine to make hockey pucks. (Getty Images)

Education and Training

For most manufacturing work, a high school diploma is desired, although it is not always necessary. New employees often receive on-the-job training from the company that hires them. Depending on the type of manufacturing operation involved, this training may last from just a few days up to several months. Some sporting goods production workers first work as apprentices at a small sporting goods manufacturer.

Outlook

As sports and fitness become more popular among health-conscious Americans, the market for sporting goods is expected to continue to grow. Exports of American-made goods may also increase in coming years.

This does not mean, however, that the number of jobs in sporting goods manufacturing will also increase. The manufacture of many kinds of sports gear is very labor-intensive, and to keep labor costs down, manufacturers have moved some of their operations to plants in other countries where workers can be paid lower wages. Advances in automation, robotics, and computer-aided manufacturing also are allowing companies to phase out certain production jobs. In the future, the need will be for employees who can program machines, supervise production, and manage resources. Workers will also be needed to test product safety and quality.

For More Information

Participate in as many sports as you can throughout your school years. Become familiar with the equipment for each sport. Research sports equipment regulations at the high school, college, and professional levels.

Sporting Goods Manufacturers Association
1150 17th Street, NW, Suite 850
Washington, DC 20036-4641
202-775-1762
info@sgma.com
http://www.sgma.com

Sports Agents

SKILLS SPOTLIGHT

What they do
Communicate ideas
Exercise leadership
Help clients and customers

Skills they need
Integrity/honesty
Social
Speaking/listening

What Sports Agents Do

Sports agents represent professional athletes in many different types of negotiations. They may represent only one athlete or many. Their main duty is to negotiate contracts, which requires great communication skills. Agents need to clearly summarize the athlete's salary and benefit demands. They have a clear idea of the athlete's future and how the contract might affect it. Agents usually represent a client during the client's entire career. Sometimes this means finding work for athletes once their athletic careers are over.

Sports agents also negotiate endorsement contracts, where the athlete sponsors a product or company in exchange for money. Endorsements and public appearances bring extra income for the athlete, but they also can create good publicity. Sports agents make sure media attention is positive and benefits the athlete. The athlete who wants to attract top endorsements and public appearances must have charisma and a good image in addition to being a top athletic performer.

Agents keep up professional and social contacts that might help clients. By developing friendly business relationships, the agent is better able to negotiate product endorsement deals. Networking is an important part of the everyday routine of sports agents.

Sports agents also give financial advice to their clients or find reliable financial advisers. Creating or finding tax shelters, investing money, and preparing for the athlete's retirement are all duties that agents routinely perform for their clients.

Other responsibilities include keeping the client happy with his or her situation, renegotiating contracts if necessary, and scheduling public appearances and media interviews.

Sports agents are in constant contact with people. They have to be aggressive and persistent in asserting the demands of their clients. They must be as comfortable

---

SCHOOL SUBJECTS
Business, Speech

MINIMUM EDUCATION LEVEL
Bachelor's degree

SALARY RANGE
$30,780 to $66,440 to $103,440

OUTLOOK
Faster than the average

OTHER ARTICLES TO READ
Literary Agents
Professional Athletes—Individual Sports
Professional Athletes—Team Sports
Sports Coaches
Sports Executives
Sports Scouts

speaking with complete strangers as they are talking to their best friends.

Education and Training

Business and mathematics courses will teach you about management and numbers. English and speech classes will develop your communication skills.

A bachelor's degree in a field such as business administration, marketing, or sports management is recommended for this field. Many people who eventually become agents also have a graduate degree in law or business. To earn a law degree, you must complete a three-year law school program after you complete at least three years of college. Most law school graduates take the bar exam, a written exam given by the state in which you want to practice.

Many sports agents who are not lawyers obtain a license or professional registration to show their commitment and integrity.

Outlook

The outlook for sports agents, in general, looks good and employment opportunities are expected to grow faster than the average through 2016. The sports industry is thriving, and there is nothing to suggest that the public's interest in it will dwindle. In fact, as cable television brings greater choices to the viewer, it is possible that less-publicized sports will gain in popularity through the increased exposure.

Sports agent Mark Steinberg (r) walks with his client Tiger Woods during a golf tournament. (AFP/Getty Images)

For More Information

Participate in school and community sports. You do not necessarily have to be an athlete, although that would help you understand the needs of your future clients. You can shag balls at tennis tournaments, be a golf caddy, or apply for ball-and-bat-assistant positions with major or minor league baseball teams. Read biographies of famous athletes to learn how they and their agents have managed their careers.

IMG—International Management Group
IMG Center, Suite 100
1360 East Ninth Street
Cleveland, OH 44114-1782
216-522-1200
http://www.imgworld.com

Sports Broadcasters and Announcers

What Sports Broadcasters and Announcers Do

Sports broadcasters and announcers share their love for sports with radio and television audiences. They must be knowledgeable of the rules, plays, and teams of the sport they are covering.

Sports broadcasters, known also as *sportscasters*, announce current athletic information, including the highlights of games, on radio or television during the sports portion of a news program. They research topics by reading sports-related news items, phoning key contacts, and interviewing athletes and coaches. In delivering their scripts, they may augment descriptions of key plays by including actual audio or video clips from the games. Sports broadcasters may also present pre- or post-game coverage during a crucial game or tournament or provide commentary for special sports features.

Sports announcers provide play-by-play details during a game. In addition, they make announcements before and during the game and introduce the starting line-ups. Often referred to as the "official voice" of the team, these announcers must have a good grasp of the detailed history of the sport covered as well as insight about the team's coaching, managing, and playing ability. Announcers must have a commanding, articulate voice and be quick to pick up on the action as it unfolds on the playing field.

Overall, sports broadcasters and announcers are very popular with their audiences and usually have charismatic and engaging personalities. Many are community celebrities and are called on to emcee sports banquets, grand openings of and special events at sporting goods stores, and other public appearances.

SCHOOL SUBJECTS
Communications, English, Physical education

MINIMUM EDUCATION LEVEL
Some postsecondary training

SALARY RANGE
$19,180 to $33,470 to $73,880

OUTLOOK
Decline

OTHER ARTICLES TO READ
Broadcast Engineers
Sports Agents
Sports Coaches
Sports Photographers
Sports Publicists
Sports Scouts
Sportswriters

Sports broadcaster Chris Meyers interviews quarterback Matt Ryan of the Atlanta Falcons. (Getty Images)

Education and Training

In high school take courses in communications, drama, English, foreign language, theater, and public speaking. Physical education courses will increase your knowledge of the rules and plays for individual sports.

Broadcasting schools offer apprenticeship training and provide excellent opportunities for making contacts in the field. In choosing any postsecondary school, carefully research the institution's accreditation status and reputation as well as its track record in placing graduates.

An associate's degree in communications, broadcasting, journalism, or physical education is recommended, while a bachelor's degree will allow you to stand out among the competition.

Sports broadcasters and announcers need training in voice and timing. They must enunciate clearly and have a strong, appealing voice. In addition, they must have a good command of the language, in particular sports jargon, practice proper grammar, and have a keen sense of timing. Specialized courses are available at the postsecondary level to hone these communication skills.

Outlook

Job opportunities for sports broadcasters and announcers are on the decline for a number of reasons. Among them are advances in technology and the consolidation of radio and television stations. Positions will open up due to retirements and job transfers.

For More Information

Begin to develop your sports broadcasting and announcing skills by volunteering to announce game plays during your school's athletic events and broadcasting highlights of the activities on the school's radio or television station.

American Sportscasters Association
225 Broadway, Suite 2030
New York, NY 10007-3001
212-227-8080
http://www.americansportscastersonline.com

National Association of Broadcasters
1771 N Street, NW
Washington, DC 20036-2800
202-429-5300
nab@nab.org
http://www.nab.org

SportsAnnouncing.com
701 Morningside Court
Heundon, VA 20170-4108
DJ@SportsAnnouncing.com
703-398-5343

 # Sports Coaches

SKILLS SPOTLIGHT

What they do
Communicate ideas
Exercise leadership
Teach

Skills they need
Decision making
Responsibility
Speaking/listening

What Sports Coaches Do

There are organized sports teams at every age level and level of competition. Children as young as four can join baseball and soccer leagues. These same children can progress through pony leagues, Little League sports, and elementary school, high school, and college teams. As adults, some may even become members of professional sports teams or play on neighborhood or work-related teams.

All of these teams need sports coaches. There are two kinds of sports coaches: head coaches and athlete coaches. *Head coaches* lead teams of athletes. *Athlete coaches* work with athletes in individual sports, such as tennis, swimming, or golf. The primary responsibility of both types of coaches is to teach and inspire players and to produce winning teams and athletes.

Coaches must know all the rules and strategies of their particular sport. They must be able to analyze the performance of their players and fit players into positions where they contribute the most to their teams. Sports coaches watch their players while they practice to see what elements of their game need improvement.

Safety is a primary concern for all coaches and instructors. They make sure athletes have the right equipment and know its correct use. A major component of safety is helping athletes feel comfortable and confident with their abilities. This entails teaching the proper stances, techniques, and movements of a game, instructing them on basic rules, and answering any questions. Coaches use videos of games to demonstrate the mistakes or deficiencies of individuals as well as well-executed plays. They also watch opponents to see what their strengths and weaknesses are so they can use this information in their own strategies.

Coaches often work with *assistant coaches*, who usually focus on one specific aspect of the sport. For example, baseball teams usually have *pitching coaches, hitting*

SCHOOL SUBJECTS
English, Physical education

MINIMUM EDUCATION LEVEL
Some postsecondary training

SALARY RANGE
$14,860 to $27,840 to $61,320

OUTLOOK
About as fast as the average

OTHER ARTICLES TO READ
Aerobics Instructors
Professional Athletes—Individual Sports
Professional Athletes—Team Sports
Recreation Workers
Sports Agents
Sports Scouts

coaches, *outfield coaches*, and *first- and third-base coaches*. Football teams have *offensive coaches*, *defensive coaches*, *linebacker coaches*, and *quarterback coaches*. All of these assistant coaches work under the direction of the head coach.

Education and Training

Many sports coaches have college degrees and experience playing college-level sports. It is possible, though, for someone with knowledge and love of a sport, excellent leadership qualities, and experience to become a coach without earning a degree.

Coaches usually work their way up through the coaching system. Some begin as assistant coaches on Little League or elementary school teams. They may eventually become head coaches on high school or college teams. The very best of these coaches go on to coach world-class athletes and professional sports teams.

Outlook

America's fitness boom has created strong employment opportunities for many peo-

Sports coaches can be important mentors to their players, offering them encouragement, giving them leadership, and teaching them about fair play. (Suzanne Tucker/Shutterstock)

ple in sports-related occupations. This occupation is expected to grow at a rate about as fast as the average through 2016. Job opportunities will be greatest in urban areas, where population is the most dense. Coaching jobs at the high school or amateur level will be plentiful. The creation of new professional leagues, as well as the expansion of current leagues, will open some new employment opportunities for professional coaches, but competition for these jobs will be very intense. There is very little job security in coaching, unless a coach can consistently produce a winning team.

For More Information

Get as much experience as you can in all sports. Try out for school-sponsored team and individual sports. Also consider community sports programs, such as baseball leagues or track and field meets sponsored by recreation commissions or park districts.

American Alliance for Health, Physical Education, Recreation and Dance
1900 Association Drive
Reston, VA 20191-1598
800-213-7193
http://www.aahperd.org

American Baseball Coaches Association
108 South University Avenue, Suite 3
Mount Pleasant, MI 48858-2327
989-775-3300
http://www.abca.org

National Association for Sport and Physical Education
1900 Association Drive
Reston, VA 20191-1598
800-213-7193
http://www.aahperd.org

Sports Equipment Managers

What Sports Equipment Managers Do

Sports equipment managers are responsible for maintaining, ordering, and inventorying athletic equipment and apparel. They deal with everything from fitting football shoulder pads to sharpening hockey skates to doing the team's laundry. Other duties include purchasing, maintenance, administration and organization, management, professional relations and education, and keeping inventory of all the equipment.

The responsibilities of equipment managers vary greatly, depending on whether they work for high schools, colleges, universities, or professional teams. Duties are also different from sport to sport, because some sports have more participants or require more equipment than others.

Sports equipment managers are responsible for ordering all the equipment (including uniforms) for their team or school's sports programs. Once the equipment arrives, they make sure that it properly fits each player. Poor fitting equipment or uniforms can cause discomfort, a lack of mobility, a reduction of vision and hearing, and even injury. After use, equipment managers keep the equipment in good working order. They inspect and clean each piece of equipment to ensure that it meets safety standards. Equipment managers are also responsible for equipment control, which includes pre- and postseason inventory, use, and storage.

Equipment managers need good communication and personnel management skills because they work with coaches, athletic directors, and their staffs. They also must be able to take criticism, be creative and responsible, have basic computer skills, and have plenty of patience.

Education and Training

High school courses that will be helpful include computer science, mathematics, and business.

SCHOOL SUBJECTS
Physical education, Technical/Shop

MINIMUM EDUCATION LEVEL
High school diploma

SALARY RANGE
$23,430 to $38,360 to $60,180

OUTLOOK
Faster than the average

OTHER ARTICLES TO READ
Athletic Directors
Athletic Trainers
Professional Athletes—Individual Sports
Professional Athletes—Team Sports
Sports Coaches
Sports Facility Managers

To become a professional equipment manager, the Athletic Equipment Managers Association suggests one of the following paths: (1) high school/GED degree and five years of paid, nonstudent employment in athletic equipment management; (2) four-year college degree and two years paid, nonstudent employment in athletic equipment management; or (3) four-year college degree and 1,800 hours as a student equipment manager.

The AEMA sponsors a professional certification program. To obtain this certification, you must be 21 years of age and be a member in good standing with the AEMA, have completed one of the three listed educational requirements, and pass a certification examination.

Outlook

Employment opportunities for sports equipment managers are expected to grow faster than the average through 2016. Opportunities will be best for college and university equipment managers. Schools are being encouraged to add more women's sports to comply with Title IX guidelines, so there is a shortage of qualified women's equipment managers. AEMA certification has also brought about greater acceptance by administrators for the need to have qualified individuals in these positions. The addition of computerized inventory programs, university-wide contracts with dealers, and the big-business atmosphere of athletics in general, has increased the demand for highly knowledgeable equipment managers.

For More Information

Serving as the equipment manager of one of your high school athletic teams or clubs will give you a great introduction to work in this field. You also may volunteer to help take care of the sports equipment for a local parks and recreation department.

Athletic Equipment Managers Association
460 Hunt Hill Road
Freeville, NY 13068-9643
607-539-6300
aema@frontiernet.net
http://www.aema1.com

National Operating Committee on Standards for Athletic Equipment
11020 King Street, Suite 215
Overland Park, KS 66210-1201
913-888-1340
http://www.nocsae.org

Former NBA player Manute Bol (l) has a hockey helmet adjusted by Indianapolis Ice equipment manager Darrin Flinchem before a charity game. (Associated Press)

Glossary

Accredited Meets established standards for providing good training and education. Usually given by an independent organization of professionals to a school or a program in a school. Compare **certified** and **licensed.**

Apprentice A person who is learning a trade by working under the supervision of a skilled worker. Often receive classroom instruction in addition to their supervised practical experience.

Apprenticeship 1. A program for training apprentices (see **apprentice**). 2. The period of time that a person is working as an apprentice, usually three or four years.

Associate degree An academic rank or title given to a person who has completed a two-year program of study at a community college, junior college, or similar institution.

Bachelor's degree An academic rank or title given to a person who has completed a four-year program of study at a college or university. Also called an undergraduate degree or baccalaureate.

Certified Meets established requirements for skill, knowledge, and experience in a particular field. Granted by organizations of professionals in their field. Compare **accredited** and **licensed.**

Commission A percentage of sales revenue that is given to the salesperson as pay, either in addition to or instead of a salary.

Community college A public two-year college that grants an associate degree. Graduates may transfer to a four-year college or university to complete a bachelor's degree. Compare **junior college** and **technical community college.**

Curriculum All the courses available in a school within a particular subject.

Degree An academic distinction given by a college or university to a student who has completed a program of study.

Diploma A certificate or document given by a school to show that a person has completed a course of study or has graduated from the school.

Doctorate (Ph.D.) The highest-level academic rank or title granted by a graduate school to a person who has completed a two- to three-year program of study at a university after receiving a master's degree.

Downsizing To reduce in size or number. Often used in the business world to describe company layoffs.

E-commerce Electronic commerce. Selling goods and/or services over the Internet.

Engineering The study of putting scientific and mathematical knowledge to practical use. Typical engineering activities include planning and managing the building of bridges, dams, roads, chemical plants, machinery, and new industrial products.

Freelancer A self-employed person who handles specific jobs under contract with companies and individuals.

Fringe benefit A monetary or service bonus (such as health insurance) given to an employee in addition to regular wages or salary. Other examples of fringe benefits include performance bonuses, pension plans, paid vacations, and life insurance.

Graduate school A school that grants master's and doctorate degrees to people who have already obtained their bachelor's degrees.

Humanities The branches of learning that are concerned with language, the arts, literature, philosophy, and history. Compare **social sciences** and **natural sciences.**

Information technology (IT) Encompasses all scientific and mathematical developments that are used to create, store, and share data such as words, photographic images, motion pictures, music, and other forms of information.

Intern An advanced student (usually with at least some college training) who is employed in a job that is intended to provide supervised practical experience.

Internship 1. The position or job of an intern (see **intern**). 2. The period of time that a person is working as an intern.

Journeyman (or **journeyworker**) A person who has completed an apprenticeship or other training period and is qualified to work in a skilled trade.

Junior college A two-year college that offers courses similar to those in the first half of a four-year college program. Graduates usually receive an associate degree and may transfer to a four-year college or university to complete a bachelor's degree. Compare **community college.**

Liberal arts Subjects that develop broad general knowledge rather than specific occupational skills. Includes philosophy, literature, the arts, history, language, social sciences, and natural sciences.

Licensed Formal permission from the proper authority to carry out an activity that would be otherwise illegal. For example, a person must be licensed to practice medicine or to drive a car. Compare **certified.**

Life sciences The natural sciences that are concerned with living organisms and the processes that take place within them (see **natural sciences**).

Major The academic field in which a student specializes and receives a college degree.

Master's degree An academic rank or title given to a person who has completed a one- or two-year program of study beyond the bachelor's level.

Natural sciences All the sciences that are concerned with objects and processes in nature. Includes biology, chemistry, physics, astronomy, and geology. Compare **humanities** and **social sciences.**

Pension An amount of money paid regularly by an employer to a former employee after he or she retires.

Physical sciences The natural sciences that are concerned with nonliving matter. Includes physics, chemistry, and astronomy.

Private 1. Not owned or controlled by the government, such as a privately held company. 2. Intended only for a particular person or group, such as a private road or a private club.

Public 1. Provided or operated by the government, such as a public library. 2. Open and available to everyone, such as a public meeting.

Regulatory Establishing rules and laws for carrying out an activity. For example, a federal regulatory agency is a government organization that sets up required procedures for how certain things should be done.

Scholarship A gift of money to a student to help offset the cost of education.

Social sciences The branches of learning that are concerned with the behavior of groups of human beings. Includes economics and political science. Compare **humanities** and **natural sciences**.

Social studies   Courses of study that deal with how human societies work. Includes civics, geography, and history.

Starting salary   Salary paid to a newly hired employee, generally less than the amount paid to a more experienced worker.

Technical college   Offers courses in both general and technical subjects and awards both associate degrees and bachelor's degrees. Compare **technical community college.**

Technical community college   Offers courses in both general and technical subjects, but only awards associate degrees. Compare **technical college.**

Technical institute   Typically offers general technical courses but does not award degrees. Technical schools that offer a broader range of subjects and award degrees are usually called technical colleges or technical community colleges.

Technical school   A general term used to describe technical colleges, technical community colleges, and technical institutes. Compare **trade school** and **vocational school.**

Technician   A worker with mechanical or scientific training who works under the supervision of scientists, engineers, or other professionals.

Typically has two years of college-level education after high school.

Technologist   A worker with specialized mechanical or scientific training who works under the supervision of scientists, engineers, or other professionals. Typically has three to four years of college-level education after high school.

Trade   An occupation that involves working with one's hands. Requires specialized training and skills.

Trade school   A public or private school that offers training in one or more of the skilled trades (see **trade**). Compare **technical school** and **vocational school.**

Undergraduate   A student at a college or university who has not yet received a degree.

Undergraduate degree   See **bachelor's degree.**

Union   An organization of workers in a particular industry or company. that works to gain better wages, benefits, and working conditions for its members. Also called a labor union or trade union.

Vocational school   A public or private school that offers training in one or more skills or trades. Compare **technical school** and **trade school.**

Wage   Money that is paid in return for work completed. Generally based on the number of hours or days worked.

Index